AfroAsian Musical Imaginaries

Of Circulations and Interconnections

AfroAsian Musical Imaginaries

Of Circulations and Interconnections

Edited by
SUMANGALA DAMODARAN

 Tulika Books

Published by

Tulika Books

44 (first floor), Shahpur Jat, New Delhi 110 049, India

www.tulikabooks.in

in collaboration with

India International Centre (IIC)

40 Max Mueller Marg, New Delhi 110 003, India

© India International Centre 2024

First edition (hardback) 2024

ISBN: 978-81-965803-7-7

Printed at Chaman Offset, Delhi 110 002

Contents

CONTENTS

Foreword

Music has always existed in the world as shared culture and as a site of circulation across time and space. Across the world, it has crossed geographical boundaries, undergoing radical transformation when audiences and practices change. Musical modes have the potential for reconfiguring cultural connections and reconstructing histories. In the process of this transformation extending from generation to generation, music evolves into new melodies, produces new aesthetic judgments, and reveals a host of political and cultural contexts.

An online colloquium at the India International Centre (IIC), Delhi, on 16–17 September 2021, brought together a panel of scholars to explore musical connections and continuities among Asian and African cultures. The International Research Division (IRD) of the India International Centre, in collaboration with the 'Re-centring AfroAsia' project, Cape Town, organized a two-day discussion on the multifaceted legacies of music and inter-regional variations, which offered new insights into connected histories.

The first session of the colloquium laid out the framework for the AfroAsia project to trace new routes through the pasts of Africa and Asia – two large parts of the world whose exchanges have been obscured by Anglo-centric perspectives. A practice of attending to aural acuities, combined with imaginative recreation, was adopted to navigate this past. The subsequent sessions dealt with the circulation of music across different regions of AfroAsia, methods of engaging with non-traditional archives, and the oral and performative. Discussions highlighted how music carries traces of migration, slavery and displacement, which percolate into oral and codified traditions, passing on memories, sparking innovations. The colloquium culminated in a demonstration of drumming traditions in South Africa and Kerala, reaffirming how music is rooted in local contexts, yet conditioned by transcultural encounters.

As with earlier conferences of the IIC–International Research Division, the questions animating the colloquium led to what the Indian philosopher D.P. Chattopadhyay has termed the 'sideways and by-ways' through which ideas and beliefs cross territorial borders.[1] This expression invites a closer look at the exchanges between nomadic and settled communities, viewing the folk and the classical not as dualities but as part of a spectrum. Such explorations are beneficial in sifting the histories sedimented in material culture and in language, and eliciting the wellsprings of creativity in local contexts.

The colloquium brought together the perspectives of practitioners and scholars on a single platform where historians, anthropologists, composers, musicologists and music therapists looked at how journeys across continents are recalled in the stories handed down generations, and associated with ritual, performance and musical instruments. The panel drew on studies of the movement of communities, occupational groups and figures of oral lore, and to these added insights gleaned from a variety of sources and methods. These included oral testimony, close reading, addressing gaps in archives, and seeking out records and conceptual frameworks in different languages. In the process, they re-emphasized the notion of identity as many-layered, evolving and multivalent. Identities contained within clan and community may shift in the context of immigrants and the nation state, but specificities of identity could be reclaimed through music.

FOREWORD

We trace back the genesis of the present volume to this important colloquium. This book offers explorations at macro- and microscales, and both empirical and discursive approaches. Memories of loss became transpersonal experiences, which one author captures in a term from musical practice (*mahaul jamaana*). And the ritual performance of *ngoma* sustained diasporic identities of the Africans from South Asia to South America. It is our hope that the ideas and propositions in the book will generate further research that goes beyond traditional divisions of east and west, and find new ways of thinking through artistic transmission, its embodiment in place, and its continuity over time.

NOTE

[1] D.P. Chattopadhyay, 'India and Asia: Parallels and Transmission', in N.N. Vohra, ed., *India and East Asia: Culture and Society*, New Delhi: Shipra Publications, 2002, p. 11.

SUDHA GOPALAKRISHNAN
Executive Director,
IIC–International Research Division

Acknowledgements

This book has come about because of the keen interest shown in the musical work of the 'Re-centring AfroAsia' project by the International Research Division (IRD) of the India International Centre (IIC), Delhi. The project, funded by the Andrew Mellon Foundation and centred at the University of Cape Town, worked in partnership with several other institutions in Africa and the Dr. B.R. Ambedkar University Delhi, between 2016 and 2021. The papers presented here shares some of the outputs of the project relating to AfroAsian musical traditions, brought into conversation with scholars and artists working in related fields.

I wish to thank Sudha Gopalakrishnan, Niharika Gupta and the IIC–IRD for organizing the colloquium that has resulted in this book. A special acknowledgement of the participation and contributions by Ari Sitas (co-director of the project and Emeritus Professor at the University of Cape Town), Brett Pyper and Dilip Menon (University of the Witwatersrand) to the discussions in the colloquium. Some of the contributions, rich as they were, could not be included because of limitations of various kinds.

To Indira Chandrasekhar, Haobam Basantarani and Manan Luthra of Tulika Books, many thanks for patience with delays in getting the manuscript ready and responding to copyediting queries.

Introduction

SUMANGALA DAMODARAN

This volume has a collection of papers presented at a colloquium, 'Afro-Asian Musical Imaginaries: Interconnected Histories across Continents', that was organized by the IIC–IRD (India International Centre–International Research Division) in collaboration with a project titled 'Re-centring AfroAsia: Musical and Human Migrations, 700–1500 AD' (henceforth RAA).[1] The RAA started from Cape Town in South Africa, and became a multi-institutional project that involved the University of the Western Cape, the University of the Witwatersrand, the University of Kwazulu-Natal, the University of Cape Town, the University of Dar es Salaam, the University of Addis Ababa and Dr. B.R. Ambedkar University Delhi, between 2016 and 2021. As part of creating a new scholarship that brings the two continents together, the project has mapped the dynamism between polities in AfroAsia in the period 700–1500 CE, and has traced urban formations and state creation, energy points, trade patterns, and the movement of people, and symbolic and material goods in the region. In the colloquium, papers presented by various scholars from the project were brought into conversation with the work of several scholars and practitioners of music who work on similar themes.[2]

The work on the RAA project started as a journey to uncover pre-colonial connections in AfroAsia using music as an entry point. That large parts of Asia and Africa have been in touch with each other over centuries, in fact over almost two millennia, through a variety of sea and land routes is known – but in relatively isolated pockets of research and across limited geographical stretches of the two continents. However, if we turn to music and associated performance forms, similarities and traces of such *longue durée* interactions can be observed that allow us to uncover historical connections between parts of the two continents in new and alternative ways.

Social scientists have been trying to get Africa out of a perennial trap constructed by European and North American scholars, which defined Africa as a geographical space without history, a space where the 'primitive' and 'primitivism' thrived, and whose societies were 'traditional', exemplars of a mechanical solidarity and, in short, ensnared everything that was non-western in exaggerated scales. Or, at best, the Africa that was defined by traditionalism was also about a distorted modernity or bad forms of modernization. Through a focus on musical forms and long-distance migrations, the RAA project has provided an alternative and innovative recasting of how Africa was in the world – and in turn how the world was in Africa – prior to European colonization, and how this involved extensive and intensive exchanges with various parts of Asia over centuries. As part of this, alongside pursuing a range of archaeological, historical and sociological questions, a notable goal of the project has been to produce contemporary musical renditions and narratives around the centuries-long historical transmission of goods, peoples and ideas across the two continents. Some papers here are based on outputs from the project that were brought into conversation with the work of scholars outside the project who participated in the colloquium.

This journey is reminiscent of a wonderful passage from Ben Okri, the Nigerian novelist based in London. To quote and to damage the quote a little bit, such work finds itself 'at the foot of a fabulous bridge':

> The bridge completely suspended in the air, held up by nothing that (we) could see, was a dazzling construct, composed entirely of mist. (We)

were bewildered by the insubstantiality of the bridge. It too seemed to be made of light, of air, of feelings. (We were) afraid to step on it lest (we) would plunge down below . . .
    'What holds the bridge (we) asked (the) guide . . .
    'Only the person crossing it', came the reply.
    'You mean that if (we were) to cross the bridge (we) must at the same time hold it up, keep it suspended? . . .
    'Yes'.
    'But how can (we) do both at the same time?'
    'If you want to cross over you must. There is no other way.'
                                                              (Okri 1995: 16)

Another quote, from Frederico Garcia Lorca, provides inspiration for the kind of work presented in this book. Lorca, in his attempt to understand flamenco music's 'duende', its passionate and tragic singing, its 'black sound' as he put it, believed that it owed its origins to 'the primitive musical systems of India'. Such music 'climbs up inside you, from the soles of the feet . . . [such a] mysterious power which everyone senses and no philosopher explains'. He further writes,

> The essential difference between cante jondo and flamenco is that the origin of the former must be sought in the primitive musical systems of India, that is, in the first manifestations of song, while the latter, a consequence of the first, cannot be said to acquire its definitive form until the eighteenth century. . . . The former is song imbued with the mysterious colour of primordial ages; the latter is relatively modern, its emotional interest eclipsed by that of the other. . . . That is to say that, cante jondo, like the primitive musical systems of India, is merely a stammer, an emission, higher and lower pitch, of the voice, a marvellous buccal undulation, that breaks out of the echoing prison of the tempered scale, will not suffer the cold rigid pentagram of our modern music and makes the hermetic flowers of semitones open in a thousand petals. (Lorca 1922: 4)

Lorca, himself an accomplished pianist, was to make recordings of the 'Deep Song' with the singer La Argentinita in the early years of the twentieth century. She was a Spanish-Argentine flamenco dancer, choreographer and singer whose actual name was Encarnacion López Julvez and who made five gramophone records with Lorca; they performed together often.

The most important question raised in the papers presented here is how music can be an important yet unusual lens through which *longue durée* connections between the continents can be unravelled, and how such scholarship and performative interactions can prise open several orthodoxies in the understanding of musical systems. Cultural connections between parts of the world that have long historical roots can be uncovered through music even when the connections have not been adequately identified or acknowledged.

In exploring the 'thousand petals' of the 'hermetic flowers of semitones', the outputs from the RAA project relating to music, some of which are presented here, relied a lot on the 'sounds like', or the nuances that a discerning ear picked up as similarities between melodies, musical structures and performative motifs. To dwell on the 'sounds like' as a methodological tool, Lorca's 'Deep Song', to use an important example, came imbued with the travels of the Roma people into southern Spain, and consists of melodies that would be classified under the Bhairavi–Bhairav family in the Indian tradition, the Hijaz *maqām* in the Arabic tradition or the Phrygian dominant scale in the western tradition. This is but one example of the uncanny resemblances that we find in melodic patterns, lyrics or instrumentation amongst many from the contemporary period that allow us to uncover migrations and connections in the *longue durée*, dating from the deep past in the pre-colonial period.

An instance is the sung version of the ballad of *Heer–Ranjha*, the popular *heer* form that is heard in the Punjab provinces of both present-day India and Pakistan. The *heer* is used to relate the love story of Heer–Ranjha, as well as to depict love and joy or to lament separation, dislocations associated with migration, social conflict and other issues that cause ruptures in society. Waris Shah, the Punjabi

Sufi poet, is said to have written the modern-day version of the Heer–Ranjha story, commonly referred to as *Heer–Waris Shah*, in the eighteenth century, and to be the creator of the canonical sung *heer* form based on the minor note-based north Indian Bhairavi rāga or the Phrygian scale/mode. While the canonical *heer* is Bhairavi-based, those who have documented it and/or sung its different versions talk about more than fifty versions of the *heer* that can be found.

The singing of the *heer* changes with the terrain and perhaps with the social histories of the areas that it covers. Closer to the Afghanistan border of Punjab in both India and Pakistan, a version is found that is based on the Bhairavi but is much less elaborate than the canonical *heer*. The story of Heer and Ranjha as well as the *heer* melodic family circulate across the regions with variations that could be attributed to time, geography and specific histories. The Bhairavi and its variants are associated with long common histories of the north-western frontiers of India and Pakistan, and extending into territories across Afghanistan, Iran and further in West Asia. In India and Pakistan alone, variants such as the Sindhi Behravi, or Sindhu Bhairavi, associate the melodies with the province of Sindh that traverses the borderlands of the two countries, marked by the Sindhu or Indus river. In south Indian music, the Bhairavi that we are referring to is called the Sindhu Bhairavi, this being an obvious reference to its association with the Sindhu river.

The Bhairavi rāga or its variants (the range of Ahir Bhairav, Bhairav, Jogiya and Basant Mukhari rāgas in the north Indian tradition) appear at many locations along the route we are describing, namely India, Pakistan, Iran, several countries in West Asia, the Balkans, North Africa and Spain. The Bhairavi is the Phrygian scale in the western musical system and close to the Hijaz *maqām* in the *maqāmat* classification system found in many parts of West Asia, Turkey and North Africa. As we move further west across the map, in Khorasan in Iran, among Khorasani musicians belonging to the nomadic Bakhtiari community, a very similar melody in the notes of the Ahir Bhairav rāga is found in the singing of another love story, that of Shirin–Khusrow. This is an example of the way in which the fascinating story of Shirin and Khusrow II, empress and emperor respectively of the late Sassanid period (fifth century CE), has come down over the centuries. From around the seventh century onwards, but particularly from the ninth century, the love story of Shirin and Khusrow came to be written about and idealized. A contemporary rendering of the story by Parvin Alipour has characteristics similar to the canonical *heer*.

The setting of the scene or mood with the interaction between the instrument and the voice is an important characteristic of Sufi singing in India and Pakistan as well as in the Alipour melody. An additional characteristic in Alipour's rendering, similar to the *heer*, is the descending melismatic or legato phrase from the fourth, through the minor third and the minor second to the first, a phrase that repeats like a code in the melody and appears to define its 'mood' as a lament.

This kind of work that begins from a 'sounds like' exercise needs a two-way reconstruction: one using performance in the contemporary period to provide us with traces of the past; and two, working through a variety of artefacts and materials from the past to imagine what music in the past might have been like and how that finds reflection in the music of the contemporary period. It is thus possible to understand soundscapes and their associational clusters as leading to links between communities and their social and ritual practices much beyond the distances that most research traverses.

Three papers in this volume employ the methodology of the 'sounds like' in exploring AfroAsian musics. Mark Aranha, in 'Melody and Identity: Following the Bake Archives', discusses how melody carries significance and value among the Jews of Kerala, also known as Cochini Jews or Cochinim. Kerala contained an important cluster of nodes in the pre-colonial Indian Ocean, and was frequented by merchants and travellers from Africa, Europe, West Asia and the east for millennia. The Cochinim, like many other communities in Kerala today, were born from these transoceanic interactions.

Aranha's methodology uses archival music available from the field recordings made by Arnold Bake in the 1930s as an entry point to explore the history, narratives and social complexities of Kerala's Jews. The analysis is based on interviews with community elders, transcriptions of archival recordings, and secondary research that he conducted during his Master's degree at the University of Cape Town between 2017 and 2019.

In 'The Body-in-Music: Musical Entrances into Historiography', Kathyayini Dash discusses the 'body-in-music' as a composite category that is central to a musical entrance into historiography. Through a discussion of *wayee*, a lament form sung by several nomadic communities across the north-western migratory corridors of Sindh, Punjab and Gujarat, she shows how histories are encoded in music, especially while working with nomadic subjectivities. Based on fieldwork done with the Bhagaadiya Jatt community of Kachchh, which has a long nomadic past traced back to the eleventh century, and having followed long migratory paths which include routes that cut across parts of Europe, Asia and Africa, she looks at the *wayee* as a musical system that was born out of the grief of exile.

Luis Gimenez Amoros, in 'From *Qaul* to *Haul* or Vice Versa: A Musical Circulation between Western Sahara and India from the Twelfth to the Fifteenth century' explores possible commonalities between the musical traditions of the *haul*, found in Western Sahara and Mauritania, the *qaul* in West Asia, and the *qawwali* of South Asia, in their formation and expansion from the twelfth to the fifteenth century. He proposes that the poetic and musical forms used in *haul* and *qaul* music resonate with the idea of musical circulation in the pre-colonial imaginary from India to Mauritania from the Islamic expansion and the revival of Greek philosophy in Persia during the ninth century. Furthermore, he explores how these musical styles were interconnected with other musical forms such as the *noubat* modal system of Andalusi music in Spain and different parts of North Africa, and the development of *maqāmat* in Baghdad. As a result of such cultural interconnectedness, this paper reveals a poetic and musical development beyond geopolitical boundaries from Western Sahara to India or vice versa.

An important dimension that was discussed in the colloquium and which is also taken up in this volume is that of focus on musical performance itself, in order to situate musical and associated performances in a dynamic, mutually informing relationship with more established modes of historical, archaeological, sociological and musicological research. Some of the papers discuss the affordances of prioritizing performance as a mode of inquiry and how this has enabled, for example, musical performance to develop a closer relationship with more established ways of knowing in the social sciences and humanities. While one needs to be cognizant of the limitations of this way of knowing too, as with any other, focusing on performativity has widened the registers in which research can been conducted. This way of knowing, then, can be located within the broader turn to performance as research (Cook 2001), and it can be suggested that they be positioned on a spectrum that might enable us to locate them somewhere between empirical expansion and disciplinary critique. Or, to be rendering musical performance intelligible (presentable, even) in terms that would be recognizable as research in a more conventional sense. For example, voice production techniques, language in lyrics, rhythms and drumming traditions are some instances where such 'traces' that indicate connections can be found through contemporary performances. Various migrations and their effects on music can thus be understood through musical encounters in the present.

In an important intervention presented in the volume, titled 'The Musical Connections of AfroAsia through the Afro-Spiritual Consciousness of *Ngoma*', Nkosenathi Ernie Koela discusses his work with the people of the Siddi community in Gujarat who are descendants of Africans from centuries before. The Siddis perform *dhammal,* a ritual performance that consists of drumming and movement along with chants/singing in a language that is interspersed with Swahili words. Based on his fieldwork in Gujarat and an exercise in learning from a master how to construct a Siddi musical bow, which is a variant of bows that come from different African traditions, Koela discusses the ways in which such contemporary exchanges can throw light on distant pasts in a live manner. Sazi Dlamini's paper, 'Ngoma Lungundu Drum in Venda Littoral Migrations: *Ngoma* in the AfroAsian and Global Black Diaspora', examines the idea of *ngoma* as a critical element of transmission, retention and deployment of musical elements in black diasporic cultures and their host environments. The term *ngoma* conceptually articulates the musical repertoires of embodied ritual performance, belief and spirituality of both African as well as far-flung transoceanic diasporic subjects. Dlamini argues that in attributing sources of their long-held spirituality and religious practices to *ngoma* (and *ngoma* links to Africa), contemporary diasporic subjects in Asia, South America, Caribbean and other oceanic islands reinforce contemporary arguments acknowledging a coeval presence of African descendants in the developing world. Further, the presence of rich cultural elements embodied in concepts such as *ngoma* in living contemporary cultures contests the historical prevalence in northern mainstream scholarship of Africa's othering in the human peopling and modernizing processes of the world. The paper discusses in detail the case of the ngoma lungundu, a drum that accompanied the Venda community on their journey to the southern part of Africa from their purported origins in the Great Lakes region of Tanzania. Venda historical narratives of migration illustrate the centrality of the drum in the continuities of Karanga-Venda clan leadership and cultural integrity as symbolized in ritual musical performance in various social and ceremonial contexts. In the reconstruction of the Venda drum from historical memory as part of the RAA project, its ritual initiation and performance, Dlamini shows how field scholarship, narratives of shared social memory and spiritual rite performance ceremonially presented as *ukuhlangabeza* can be an example of knowledge production that is rooted in performance and memory.

Paroma Ghose, in the paper 'Asian and African Imaginaries and their Encounters in Rap in France (1981–2012); presents a different dimension of music as it emerges from diasporic communities. She argues that Europe, and the extensive legacy that it left in the wake of its multinational colonial empires, has not only governed the geopolitical realities of the past few centuries, but also reverse-engineered the discourse on this past so that the study and general understanding of both history and memory continue to hold Europe at their centre. It has thereby over-ridden the connections and exchanges or encounters that took place between non-European societies before, during and after the age of European empires. In her work, Europe, or France to be more precise, is where those of varying migratory backgrounds encounter each other. Not only are migrants in France brought together by its geographic contours, but also by the physical spaces they share and, often, the social classes that these inadvertently define. Most of all, they share the periphery of societal existence. In other words, they are constantly ostracized by society for appearing to be 'incongruous' to what is practically accepted as the 'national norm' of the citizenry, even if this is nowhere clearly defined. Rappers form a fascinating microcosm of this ostracized 'other' in France, and their powerful and popular lyrical discourse provides a critical insight into the realities of those who wish to belong to the nation-state but to whom the nation-state does not reciprocate this loyalty. Based on extensive fieldwork with French rappers of Asian and African origin, Ghose brings out the expression of (severe) discontent with the societal status quo because of a continued experience of discrimination and the coalescence of people of diverging origins and/or descent in the form of a united collective whom the rappers are representing.

Manoj Kuroor's paper, 'The Drumming Tradition of South India with Special Reference to the Percussion Art Forms of Kerala', describes various drumming traditions from Kerala and their performance features. Arguing that the case of Kerala is unique, where percussion is perhaps more important and developed than vocal music traditions, in the sense of complexity and stylization, he draws attention to the rhythmic structure and variety, variations in tempo and improvisational techniques in different drumming traditions such as *chendamelam* and *panchavadyam*. The papers in this volume, it is hoped, will provide a glimpse into less explored ways of using music as an entry point to understanding AfroAsian musical imaginaries and uncovering the long historic connections between the two continents.

NOTES

[1] This introductory chapter has drawn from the discussion in the first session of the colloquium, with contributions by Ari Sitas, Emeritus Professor, University of Cape Town, and Brett Pyper, University of the Witwatersrand.

[2] The following papers which were presented during the colloquium do not form a part of the present volume: Janie Cole, 'Ethiopia in India: Music and Migration in the Early Modern Indian Ocean World'; Dilip Menon, 'Language, Music, and Histories across the Ocean'; Tejaswini Niranjana, 'Vocal Music and the Performance of Modernity'; Brett Pyper, 'Performing as Knowing: Recentring Performance in the "Re-centring AfroAsia" Project'; Imagi Sanga, 'Encountering Imperial Forces with Ngoma: Swahili Letters and the Archiving of Sonic Cultures in Tanzania'; and Ari Sitas, 'Creating a New Scholarship in Music'.

REFERENCES

Cook, N. (2013), *Beyond the Score: Music as Performance*, New York: Oxford University Press.

Lorca, F.G. ([1922] 2008), 'Importancia histórica y artística del primitivo canto Andaluz llamado "Cante Jondo"' (Historical and Artistic Importance of the Primitive Andalusian Song Called 'Cante Jondo'), lecture delivered in Granada, 19 February 1922, English translation by A.S. Kline 2008, available at https://www.poetryintranslation.com/PITBR/Spanish/DeepSong.php.

Okri, B. (1995), *Astonishing the Gods*, London: Phoenix.

1

Melody and Identity

Following the Bake Archives

MARK ARANHA

My introduction to the Jews of Kerala was through a collection of recordings at the Archives and Research Center for Ethnomusicology (ARCE), Gurgaon.[1] These were made in 1938 by Dutch musicologist Arnold Bake, prior to the formation of the state of Israel and the resultant emigration of much of Kerala's Jewish population. The recordings were not accompanied by any notes other than a basic catalogue.

Though I was equipped with some contextual knowledge – the idea of the Indian Ocean as a pre-colonial network of exchange and

30.4	⨂	Jewish Community songs, Psalm 29.	Cochin	7/4/38
30.5	⨂	"	"	" , morning hymn.	"	"
30.6	⨂	"	"	, Purim.	"	"
30.7	⨂	"	"	, Oanam.	"	"
30.8	⨂	" Jews).	"	, Rejoicing (black	"	"
30.9	⨂	"	"	, Prophet Jesaya, 57 days of atonement.	"	"
30.10	⨂	"	"	,Levitious (chapt.16).	"	"

An excerpt from Bake's catalogue
Source: Archives and Research Center for Ethnomusicology (ARCE), Gurgaon.

25

Kerala as one of its important cosmopolitan regions – my first instinct was to approach the material purely as a musician before using that information. As I listened to the seven recordings, there was one that caught my ear as undeniably distinct. Intriguingly, this was the recording that contained the words 'black Jews' in parentheses.

The annotation must have held some significance for Bake to include it in his very brief item description. Who were these 'black Jews'? And who were the others, if not explicitly identified?

A BRIEF HISTORY OF THE JEWS IN KERALA

Local legend has it that Jews were already present in Kerala when St Thomas the Apostle is supposed to have arrived there, in the first century CE.[2] Hebrew signatures in the Kollam copperplates of 850 CE give us the first inscriptional evidence of Jews in Kerala (Narayanan 1972: 37). Another significant inscription is the royal grant of 72 aristocratic rights to an international merchant guild, Anjuvannam, and its Jewish leader, Isuppu Irappan, in Muyirikkodu in 1000 CE (ibid.: 25).[3] Thereafter, we have various accounts that point to a Jewish presence in Kerala from the eleventh to the fifteenth century (Segal 1983: 228–29). Most of these Jewish visitors and settlers would have been of Egyptian and West Asian origins, including Yemeni and Baghdadi (Malekandathil 2001: 240).

Pre-colonial Kerala gained a reputation as a warm and hospitable place for Jews. A number of Jews displaced by the inquisition in Spain and Portugal started to arrive there around the sixteenth century. They gained such favour with the king of Cochin that he allowed them to build a synagogue on his palace grounds. This constituted the beginnings of what would become the Paradesi Jewish community.[4] All previously existing Jews in Kerala, regardless of ethnicity or tradition, were lumped together into a single category, namely Malabari Jews. The Malabaris accounted for at least seven congregations, five of them outside the island of Cochin. The map on the facing page shows the locations of all known synagogues in

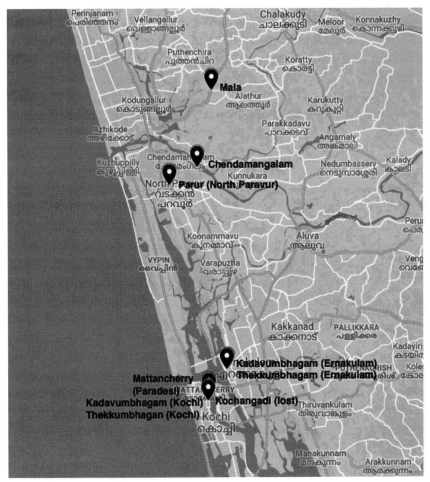

All known locations of synagogues in Kerala
Source: Aranha (2021): 117.

Kerala: one Paradesi synagogue is in Mattancherry and the remaining are Malabari synagogues.

Despite the fact that they far outnumbered their more prosperous counterparts, the Malabaris were relatively under-represented in the literature. Some of them allege that their historical narratives, stories of migration and other traditions were distorted and appropriated by the Paradesis (Aranha 2021: 104–06). Throughout the colonial period, European visitors tended to restrict their visits to the island of Cochin, and focused their studies on the Paradesi Jews.

Within a few decades of their arrival, the Paradesi Jews began to construct a race-based identity for themselves as white Jews, woven in with myths of ancient origin (Gamliel 2009: 56; Schorsch 2004: 195–96). This was readily reproduced by visiting scholars and writers. In 1687, a Jew visiting from Amsterdam, Mosseh Pereira de Paiva, who was quite taken with the Paradesis, published a document titled 'Relacion delas Noticias delos Judios de Cochin'. This became the European point of reference for the 'Jews of Cochin', as de Paiva called them. The Paradesis had presented him with the copperplates of Joseph Rabban as proof of their authenticity and ancient lineage. De Paiva did not bother to question how they could have been related to Joseph Rabban if they had only arrived after the expulsion. Instead, he proceeded to list the families of the community in his census, making sure to label the important ones 'B' for 'brancos' or 'whites'; as for the 'black Jews', he alleged that they were descendants of the slaves of the Jews of Cranganore (de Paiva 1687; Schorsch 2008: 75).

Schorsch explains that this 'whiteness' was derived more from assertions of power and authenticity than physical phenotype. He points out that de Paiva tried to attribute the darker complexion of the 'brancos' to the Indian sun, denied any possible miscegenation, and highlighted the exclusion of the 'Malabaris' from the Paradesis' prayers. All this indicates a synthesis of the constructs of caste and race (Schorsch 2008: 67, 73–76). The terminology of 'white Jews' and 'black Jews' endured unchecked in the literature till the first half of the twentieth century, even finding its way into Bake's catalogue.

Restudying the Bake Archives

Nazir Jairazbhoy and Amy Catlin-Jairazbhoy conducted a re-study of Bake's work in 1984. Jairazbhoy had previously been Bake's student and research assistant at the School of Oriental and African Studies, London during 1956–63. He took up this re-study alongside his wife Amy Catlin-Jairazbhoy in an effort to replicate Bake's findings and explore his methodologies (Jairazbhoy 1991: 1). To study the Jewish recordings the researchers visited Cochin, where they were hosted by the Koder family, the leaders of the Paradesi community.[5] They tried to find people who might remember Bake's visit, and perhaps identify and contextualize some of the songs. Their work confirmed that Bake had recorded songs from not only the Paradesi congregation, but also some by Malabari Jews. However, it seems that they did not venture into the Ernakulam synagogues or cover any Malabari Jewish sources on this trip (Jairazbhoy 1984: 92).

During my visits to Cochin and Ernakulam in 2018, I focused on Malabari sources. This enabled me to gather different information on the same recordings, and in one case, to identify a previously unidentified song. I was also fortunate to be invited to a special Sefer Torah ceremony for the Kadavumbhagam synagogue in Ernakulam.

By the 1970s, most of the congregation here had left for Israel. The remaining Jews could not put together the *minyan* (quorum) of ten Jewish men who could read the Torah, and the community could no longer hold regular prayers here. While other Malabari synagogues fell into disrepair, Elias Josephai, son of the Kadavumbhagam synagogue's *chazzan*,[6] took up the task of preserving the synagogue. Funds were not easy to come by, but he managed to maintain the premises by running a nursery and aquarium business named Cochin Blossoms within it.

The Hachnasat Sefer Torah ceremony celebrates the presentation of a new Torah scroll to the synagogue. It was especially significant for Elias and the Kadavumbhagam synagogue as it marked the completion of the synagogue's renovation forty-six years after it was

A full house at the Sefer Torah ceremony of the Kadavumbhagam synagogue, Ernakulam
Source: Aranha (2021): 133.

closed in 1972. A group of Malabari Jews travelled from Israel for the event, and they gave me some time to interview and record them.

IDEAS OF MELODY AND IDENTITY

It became apparent from these conversations that melodic aesthetics hold significant value for the Cochinim. They took pride in telling me which tunes were unique to their congregation or to the Jews of Kerala. In Israel, melodies for the same text could be quite different depending on tradition – a Moroccan melody would be different from a Yemeni or an Ashkenazi melody. Among the Cochinim, melodies seemed to vary even between their own congregations.

One of my respondents was an excellent singer. His voice stood out in a chorus because of the way he embellished the melodies. The skeletal notes were the same, but the ornamentation was deliberate and beautiful. When I asked him about this, he said:

> It's very simple. In each place, even here, you are influenced by where you are living. Even here, in two synagogues, I want to show you that I'm different from you. Why do you have two synagogues? Because you are divided about the property and many other things. . . . If I hear a good song, I want to finish with this. And if you are the father, your son heard it. And the other father, he wants to show the way he finishes it.

He was describing the embellishment on the ends of his melodic lines. His father belonged to the Chendamangalam synagogue before he moved to Israel, and that is where he learned to sing these lines. He told me another story about how the melody of the *mussaf* prayers became a matter of dispute in one of the synagogues:[7]

> We have a nice story about when you pray . . . we call it *mussaf*. For almost a hundred or maybe a thousand years, we sang it in one way. Then 150 years ago, some people arrived from Europe and they said no, we should pray in another version. That caused in the Cochin Jewry a fight for almost five years, and they prayed in two shifts. One started at

6 [am] and finished at 8, and the other started at 8 and finished at 10. But because these . . . said the other version, this fellow continued the prayer in his version. About these things they were fighting. All this among the religious . . .

Another respondent sang two versions of a Yom Kippur song – a Malabari version that was slow and deliberate, guided by the syllables of the text, followed by a rushed Paradesi version where he squeezed the syllables into even meter. He then said, 'Our [Malabari] tune is a little . . . you can hear, more beautiful, little stretched out. . . . The original is always original. You understand? . . . You cannot get the hundred per cent out of the copy.'

Jairazbhoy and Catlin-Jairazbhoy recorded a similar complaint from the Paradesi Jews. One of their hosts criticized the rendition on Bake's recording of the tune 'Today is Purim.'[8] He claimed the tune was composed by his grandfather, and that it should not have been sung 'so sadly' but should sound 'merry' (Catlin-Jairazbhoy 1984: 48, 50).

There were also comments on melodic motion and range. Two respondents independently pointed out that Cochini melodies were sung in a limited range and tended to have smaller steps, as opposed to other Jewish traditions with large intervallic leaps. One complained that Ashkenazi melodies would go too high or too low for them to sing. Bake's seven recordings agreed with these descriptions. Each of the seven tunes was sung within a single octave, and most of them stuck to conjunct (linear, step-wise) motion.

I found in my analysis that the Paradesi tunes maintained a single mode or scale, but two of the three Malabari tunes switched modes. To stay within a mode would mean that scale degrees are not altered, whereas to switch modes would mean that one or more degrees of the scale may change during the song, implying the use of more than one mode. The Malabari tunes tended to alter some of these scale degrees (Aranha 2021: 169–75). This could imply a possible basis in a musical tradition such as *maqām*, where modal mixture is a common device.[9]

CONCLUSION

My study is not a comprehensive survey of the Jewish music of Kerala. However, from the few interviews and anecdotes presented here, it may be inferred that melody is valued as a marker of identity among the different Malabari Jewish congregations as well as the Paradesis. Their renditions are a conscious choice and a source of pride for them.

Where melody is important enough to be a valid object of criticism or appraisal within the community, it should be of interest to the cultural historian. It is possible that the perceptible stylistic differences among Bake's recordings of the Cochinim reflect different historical traditions and paths of migration. In the process of tracing connections across borders, musical analysis can give us an extra dimension to operate in.

NOTES

[1] My methodology used archival music as an entry point to exploring the history, narratives and social complexities of Kerala's Jews. The final output is based on interviews with community elders, transcriptions of archival recordings, and secondary research I conducted during my postgraduate degree at the University of Cape Town between 2017 and 2019.

[2] See blog on P.M. Jussay for more on Kerala's Jewish and Christian oral traditions, https://pmjussay.tripod.com/id21.html

[3] The merchant Isuppu Irappan is better known as Joseph Rabban, while Muyirikkodu was an important port known to the Romans as Muziris.

[4] If we go by Visscher's letters written in 1723, the Paradesi (or 'white') Jewish settlement in Mattancherry would have been formed around the year 1521; he writes that they have been living there for '202 years' (Visscher 1862: 115). It is likely that Visscher is going by some oral tradition as he does not reveal any source or evidence for these dates.

[5] Nazir Jairazbhoy and Amy Catlin-Jairazbhoy published a film and monograph titled *The Bake Restudy in India 1938–1984*. However, this did not cover the re-study of the Jewish recordings. The information from their trip to Cochin was sourced from their field notes, which may be accessed at the Archives and Research Center for Ethnomusicology (ARCE) in Gurgaon, Haryana.

[6] *Chazzan*, also *hazan*, is the cantor who leads a synagogue's congregation in prayer.

[7] *Mussaf* (pl. *mussafin*) are additional prayers sung on a Sabbath or on special

days. See https://www.chabad.org/library/article_cdo/aid/939953/jewish/Laws-of-the-Musaf-Prayers.htm

[8] Purim, or the festival of lots. See https://www.chabad.org/holidays/purim/article_cdo/aid/645309/jewish/What-Is-Purim.htm

[9] The transcriptions for Bake's Jewish recordings are available in my Master's dissertation (Aranha 2021).

BIBLIOGRAPHY

Aranha, M. (2021), 'Jews and Mappilas of Kerala: A Study of Their History and Selected Song Traditions', MMus dissertation, University of Cape Town, South Africa.

Catlin-Jairazbhoy, A. (1984), 'Bake Restudy Notes by Amy Catlin', Collection no. 1, 'Nazir and Amy Jairazbhoy', Archives and Research Centre for Ethnomusicology, Gurgaon.

de Paiva, M. Pereira (1687), 'Relacion Delas Noticias Delos Judios De Cochin', electronic resource, Embiada Por El Sr. Mosseh Pereira De Pavia, New York: Columbia University Libraries, https://archive.org/details/ldpd_11554177_000

Gamliel, O. (2009), 'Jewish Malayalam Women's Songs', PhD dissertation, Hebrew University, Jerusalem.

Jairazbhoy, N.A. (1984), 'NAJ Diary 1984', Collection no.1, 'Nazir and Amy Jairazbhoy', Archives and Research Centre for Ethnomusicology, Gurgaon.

_____ (1991), _The Bake Restudy in India 1938–1984_, video monograph, Van Nuys, California: Apsara Media for Intercultural Education.

Malekandathil, P. (2001), 'The Jews of Cochin and the Portuguese: 1498–1663', _Proceedings of the Indian History Congress_, vol. 62, pp. 239–55.

Menon, K.P. Padmanabha, T.K. Krishna Menon and Jacobus Canter Visscher (1929), _A History of Kerala: Written in the Form of Notes on Visscher's Letters from Malabar_, vol. 2, Ernakulam: Cochin Government Press.

Narayanan, M.G.S. (1972), _Cultural Symbiosis in Kerala_, Trivandrum: Kerala Historical Society.

Schorsch, J. (2004), _Jews and Blacks in the Early Modern World_, Cambridge: Cambridge University Press.

_____ (2008), 'Mosseh Pereyra De Paiva: An Amsterdam Portuguese Jewish Merchant Abroad in the Seventeenth Century', in Y. Kaplan, ed., _The Dutch Intersection: The Jews and the Netherlands in Modern History_, Leiden and Boston: Brill, pp. 63–86.

Segal, J.B. (1993), _A History of the Jews of Cochin_, London, England: Vallentine Mitchell.

Visscher, J.C. (1862), _Letters from Malabar; by Jacob Cantor Visscher; Now first translated from the original Dutch; To which is added an Account of Travancore, and Fra Bartolomeo's Travels in That Country_, translated by Heber Drury, Madras.

2

The Body-in-Music

Musical Entrances into Historiography

KATHYAYINI DASH

The state of Gujarat in India is home to a seamless white desert – the Rann as it is known in the vernacular, grasslands or Banni, and some important ancient port towns. A range of marginalized nomadic communities have settled here over the centuries. These groups have deep-rooted and old musical lineages that comprise songs, sung folk tales, community stories and narratives. The histories of these communities are available through these songs, folklore, beliefs and family histories. The characters of the folk tales and songs are said to be linked by family lineages to individuals or communities singing them today. Their migration histories are interconnected with a thriving Bhakti music tradition that emerged from these communities, a great deal of which is yet to be archived.[1] Stories of love and travel, legends of seafaring/fishermen communities, stories of weather and celebration occupy the regions of their memory and music, and these became their language of history.

My focus in this paper is on the entry points to history afforded by a particular genre of music, the *wayee*, that is sung by the Bhagaadiya Jath community. I will attempt to show how a reading of the *wayee*, in terms of its affective value and materiality, paves the way for musical practice to be seen as a mode and a site of historiographical material. Further, I will briefly touch upon three concepts derived from musical practice – namely, *swar bithana, riyaas* and *mahaul jamaana*, which, loosely translated, could mean 'seating the (musical) note', '(musical) practice or training' and 'building of atmosphere', respectively – and show how these concepts can expand beyond the disciplinary boundaries of music and musical genres, and become historiographical modes of enquiry located in performance practice.

The *wayee* appears to operate with emotional registers of grief. It involves a retelling of the history of devotion that has emerged from histories of grief within communities that carry them in their devotional legacy. These layers of historical–musical codes could be a means to map where they came from, and to remember a different and far-off yet intimate world. Music becomes the carrier of community memories of pain and loss. My central assumption here is that this pain of singing resonates with a social history of the pain of a people and, within this context, a nomadic civilization. Memory becomes the body in music. Music becomes remembering, a carrier of pain and loss. These histories of mourning and separation are brought forth every time they are sung in the present. In other words, such performances can be characterized as embodied histories.[2]

How can such embodied historical narratives be located? When one moves away from the archival impulse, in what kinds of forms and shapes does embodied history present itself? How does one think through the intricate layers of history that are encoded in oral/aural narratives and forms of music? In this paper, I will attempt to think through the manner in which musical performance embodies the past particularly through an examination of the concepts of *swar bithana, riyaas* and *mahaul jamaana* – loosely translated, they could mean 'seating the (musical) note', '(musical) practice or training' and 'the building of an atmosphere', respectively.

My attempt to explore these concepts draws substantially on theories of embodiment. The reason for this is that all three concepts have the body as the site and point of access. This perspective views the body, especially the body in performance, as that which shapes historiographical material in particular *ways* (here we focus on music) and holds space for the possibility that certain kinds of histories *show themselves* in the practice of these embodied forms of performance. These theories of embodiment would help us read performance as embodied sites of social as well as historical engagement. Further, such an approach would enable us to understand the 'affective infra-structure' that scaffolds performance.[3] Performance, here musical performance, is thus recognized as both a carrier of historical memory and a structure of feeling (see Williams 1977; Sharma and Tygstrup, eds 2015).

The question, then, is how does one unpack this historical baggage of performances using theories of embodiment? How can performance be made to function as a methodology for explicating affective infra-structures? There could be many entry points to thinking about embodiment, of which I am particularly interested in the intersection between the question of embodiment and the practice of performance. Each of these entry points offers a method of thinking through the modalities of performance/practice. Shaun Gallagher's (2013, 2017) idea of body-schemas could perhaps serve as a useful pointer. In his article 'Theory, Practice and Performance' (Gallagher 2017), he discusses the various ways in which the concept of body-schemas has been engaged. Moving away from cognitivism and beginning from an anti-Cartesian, non-dualist premise, he takes us through two primary perspectives within the embodied cognition field – the extended mind and the enactivist models of thought. The extended mind approach understands body-schemas to extend to incorporate tools and instruments. It views the mind not as something internally residing but as extending into the environment to incorporate tools and instruments entrenched in habit. The mechanisms of cognition, according to this extended mind approach, therefore include 'pieces of environment' (ibid.: 108). The enactivist model of embodied cognition is more phenomenologically inclined. It understands perception to be 'action-oriented' and the mind to be 'distributed across the body and environment, to the extent that the body and environment are dynamically coupled' with biology, affect and environment shaping 'the constitution of consciousness and cognition, in an irreducible way', such that these processes and factors have a 'permeating effect on cognition' (ibid.: 109).

Following Gallagher, it becomes apparent that the processes of materializing history are both within and beyond the edges of the body. Understood this way, in the light of both the approaches, it can be seen that there is a concerted move across both these models to break away from the internal–external binary of body and environment. This speaks closely to the way subjectivity is understood. It can also be seen how philosophical, sociological and historiographical enquiries can be positioned around the body–world relationship within the current emerging discourse on embodiment in the field of performance (practice).

The field of performance practice helps significantly in explicating the body–world relationship, since both the procurement of knowledge and the form of knowledge lie in the doing of it. I echo Diana Taylor's insistence that performance becomes a mode of remembering, and can transmit knowledge, memory and a sense of identity (Taylor 2003: 2). She pushes for a need to create a shift from 'the written to embodied culture, from discursive to the performatic' (ibid.: 16), driven by the materiality of presence that 'enacts embodied memory' (ibid.: 20). Such a framework helps move beyond the apparent characteristic of ephemerality that is commonly assigned to the medium of performance, and in turn creates an impetus to push interdisciplinary, practice-based scholarship into novel territories of doing history.

My study of the *wayee* is mediated by my training in Hindustani classical music as well as recent collaborations with musicians from South Africa. I use a 'practice as research' (PaR) methodology and framework as a bridge between my study of the *wayee* and my own engagement with the sonic. The PaR methodology and framework, I believe, can help one grapple with these particular grammars of histories that lie in the *way* they are told, the *way* they are sung.

The PaR methodology begins with a hunch, which is different

from a hypothesis. A hypothesis pre-empts an end form and is driven by the impulse to retrieve that which exists, be it hidden or out front. A hunch, on the other hand, follows what Tim Ingold (2011a, 2011b) has termed 'wayfinding', which is, very simply put in the context of research, the following of a route as it emerges and the forming of a map as and when the routes accumulate, wherein the outcome is perceived as a punctuation in the creative research process. This shift of the end form to a punctuation is not insignificant and opens out a crucial headway into the work of historiography. What this does is provoke a rethinking of the sites of historical material and, in turn, the modes of historical enquiry. Where one looks for history, and how one looks for these histories, undergoes a productive re-evaluation.

Reading the *Wayee*

The Bhagaadiya Jath community of Kachchh has a long nomadic past that can be traced to the eleventh century. They have a broken and dispersed subjectivity of following long migratory paths which include routes that cut across parts of Europe, Asia and Africa, including Romania, Tunisia, Greece, Iran, Persia, Egypt, Tanzania, Somalia, Balochistan and Sindh, and are located in their present place as construction labourers in Bhagaadiya in the Banni region and in parts of the coastal regions of Kachchh where some of them settled down after the 1947 Partition of India and Pakistan.

The *wayee* is a musical system that was born out of the grief of exile. Today, the Bhagaadiya Jath community has only one surviving family that, according to them, sings the *wayee* in the same form as it was created in the seventeenth century by Shah Abdul Latif Bhitai.[4] It is said that Shah Abdul Latif, burdened by the taunts of the world, went into self-exile and separated himself from his lover. As he was grieving at leaving his village and his lover, notes of the *wayee* emanated from him. He is said to have shaped the notes from various screams and sounds produced out of his grief. With these notes he wove smaller systems of music called *sur*s. He wove thirty-six *surs* that told thirty-six stories of grief emerging from a variety of communities that he travelled with, that are today recognized as lower-caste communities. This system of music is sung only with prior preparation, and is an extremely exhausting and painful form of music; it weaves a grave and intense atmosphere.[5]

Music is used in some cultural traditions, such as the *wayee*, to structure feelings (Sharma and Tygstrup, eds 2015). Historicities encoded in these systems are preserved in an embodied and bodily manner. I draw upon Sara Ahmed's (2004) idea that there is not one general emotion that people feel – and that emotions or feelings are neither things inside the body needing to be expressed, nor do they lie outside having certain effects somewhere inside. She designates a sliding and sticking characteristic to emotions that move between individual and collective bodies. Musical systems like the *wayee*, because of the historical lineage, hold certain affective intensities that accumulate across a *longue durée* of time, and that can be activated and shared by creating certain atmospheres when sung in particular ways. This would imply that although emotions and feelings are involved in the making of the subject by sliding in between individual and collective bodies, there are performative and embodied ways in which these feelings are archived at the site of the body. Therefore, I would maintain that it is possible to locate these emotions within the infra-structure of music. The body becomes both the site and the medium through which such emotions can be tapped, seen, read and experienced. Nevertheless, this would place a demand on places and institutions of the archival to expand the scope of imagining the forms and materiality of historical material appearing in the non-discursive domain. The *wayee* is an example that shows us that musical form slides between the individual body of Bhitai and the collective body of the Bhagaadiya Jaths along an infra-structure of grief that embeds itself in the musical form while being woven together across long durations of time. This would mean that the musical form, which does not exist without the performing body, accumulates layers of time and historical meaning through the process of singing the *wayee* in the present. This makes the body-in-music a site of historiography and musical practice, a potential historical conduit. Here, I would like to work out the body-in-music across the concepts of *swar bithana* and *riyaas*, which point to the process of embodiment that musical practice involves, and *mahaul jamaana*, the building of a musical atmosphere, ripe with the potential of establishing a musical experience that pushes us into a tense present laden with the past.

SWAR BITHANA AND RIYAAS

Reflecting on my own practice in relation to forms such as the *wayee*, I present here an account of the embodiment of history noted after a *riyaas* (daily singing practice) session.

When you sing, you remember.

When you sing a note, you feel your chest quiver. Then that quiver travels down when you go lower and surges up to your head when you hit the high notes.

You know you are doing it right when sometimes, as you practise, it seems your head might explode or your vocal cords would tear. But they don't. The body endures through the musical labour, and pulls through the painful processes of singing till it embodies the note, through constant memorizing. The remembering of this note shapes your insides so much so that after a point, the strenuous quivers become a deliberate flow, guided seamlessly by the practised memory of the note.

The note is embodied differently by different systems of music. Passing down from generation to generation, travelling through bodies to regions, pushing through the ravages of time, the embodied note becomes historically mobile. It moves into the past and this history resurrects itself whenever it is sung in the present. The note is preserved in the act of remembering – doing music becomes remembering.

The note remembers.

(Kathyayini Dash, personal notes, 6 February 2020)

Swar bithana translates into giving the note residence, and is used in the context of learning music across canonical and some folk forms of Indian music. The scope of this paper does not allow for an extensive discussion of the metaphysical aspects of embodying a note. But even an initial exploration of the practice of *swar bithana*, where the teacher places the note in the throat of the student, which leads to the practice of *riyaas* where the student rehearses the note until its placement finds a stable point in various parts of the body, are significant concepts that resonates with my proposition that the musical note gives residence to certain experiences that are at once personal and historical. Therefore, while the learning of the musical form may be a personal process, choice or eventuality, it is simultaneously a social and cultural transmission of affect. Not in the sense of a golden pot of hereditary knowledge that is handed down along a genealogy, but of a golden pot that is perforated and constantly permeated by the present and multiple historical presences. This transmission occurs both from teacher to student and between performer and listener.

If a note can be given residence in the body, it renders the note as incredibly corporeal and physical; yet the effects of the note, when given proper residence within the body and when sung in whatever system of music, can possibly give rise to the creation and materialization of an affective and intensified atmosphere (*mahaul*).

My key assumption at this point of my research is to suggest that histories of grief can indeed be read as embodied through the material of music in a way that constructs and consolidates 'affective infra-structures'. This could lead towards arriving at various affective forms and ways of archiving the living past through practice that can potentially explicate and rewrite newer histories over hegemonic pasts, emerging from the margins.

MAHAUL JAMAANA

The *wayee*, in form and as practice, provokes one to look at the musical system beyond being a medium of expression, but rather as a cultural transmission of affect by embodying the form of music. Through the practice of these forms of music there occurs a carrying over, an encoding of history, across this dispersed nomadic body. The memory of the dispersed existence of this collective body (the Jaths) is accessed during the performance of the musical system of *wayee* and enables the dispersal of the individual body (the Jath singers, Shah Abdul Latif Bhitai followers, Mitho Khan and others).[6] 'Unfelt' pain that belongs to the community (the collective and composite body) is relived and resurrected through the voice and the *tamburo* in the present nomadic body (the individual body) via the act of remembering. A sensual and palpable atmosphere called *mahaul* is created that seems to telescope pain from the past, providing ground to present communal and individual suffering. Together this generates an atmosphere of grief that is created by the music and is immediately palpable to the listener. Although this *mahaul* is created by and emanates from the performer, the immersive atmosphere is only built along with an immersed listener. The phrase 'mahaul jamaana' used in Indian musical language translates into 'solidifying the atmosphere' or 'giving residence to the atmosphere', which has been able to move or have an affective and apparent impact on the listener. The *mahaul* cannot be brought together but comes together. I would like to think of the *mahaul* as a site where we can see or experience: (i) the work of the note at play extending out of particular processes of transmission that begin to attain a spatial dimension; and (ii) a corporeal and palpable feeling of having been moved by the presences created by the weaving of the musical form, the rendition of the form by the performer and the reception of the form by the listener.

Reading the historical within this site is a simultaneous yet parallel process that needs to be layered with a palpable and musically aware experience of the present. This musical awareness is not a product of specialization in a given form of music but is a state created within any listener, given that the *mahaul* is established. The *mahaul* is not a guaranteed experience like that of a successful science experiment where once established, it remains that way. The creation or establishment of the *mahaul* is based on a complex variety of factors that are very sensitive to change, which I believe can be slowly unpacked through consistent PaR-based enquiries.

These brief insights into the potential of musical practice as an entry into historiography are enough to point to embodied histories as indeed being present, albeit in dynamic and enmeshed forms, and processes of historical formation that call for an expansion of frameworks and lenses, deriving from interdisciplinary research practices and a deeper investigation into the historical potential of presence in performance practice.

Ideas and concepts like *swar bithana, riyaas* and *mahaul jamaana* open out space to suggest that there are certain procedures which can be developed out of performance methodologies that build ways of framing and reading the transaction of affect/emotion, which in my case is to understand grief as a 'trope' and structuring device, and provide lenses with which to make apparent pre-colonial, marginalized and nomadic histories.

NOTES

[1] Traditional accounts of the Bhakti tradition in India say that the movement emerged in the eighth century in the south of India and later travelled to the north roughly between the twelfth and the sixteenth centuries. Some historians have described it as a social reformation within Hinduism, and have argued that it provided an individual-focused alternative path to spirituality regardless of one's caste by birth or gender. Others have looked at it as a revival, as a reworking and recontextualization of ancient Vedic traditions. Groups such as the Marwaras, the Meghwals and the Vadas, among many other such communities of Kachchh, with a strong and very old musical lineage of Bhakti music appear to have a distinctive and not yet formally discussed relationship with the mainstream Bhakti tradition, not least because of their 'low'-caste nomadic past. For accounts of Bhakti, see Hawley (2015), and Hawley, Novetzke and Sharma, eds (2019).

[2] These are observations and inferences collected and made based on the field-work I conducted for the Re-centring AfroAsia project between 2018 and 2020. These are currently in the process of being transcribed for my doctoral thesis.

[3] 'Affective infra-structure' is a proposition I make in my ongoing doctoral thesis that combines perspectives from affect studies, cultural studies, performance and the visual arts to enable the explication and ability to read historical processes and formations that otherwise escape discipline-centric scholarly analysis.

[4] The verses that are sung (in the *wayee*) were first orally narrated by Shah Abdul Latif Bhitai in speech and song that are compiled in the form of a Sufi treatise called *Shah Jo Risalo* (roughly translating to 'The Shah's message'). The *Risalo* emerged gradually from various collections of verses that Shah Latif produced during his lifetime, recorded by his disciples (Shackle, ed. and trans. 2018: ix). The verses, called *bheth*, have a specific rhythmic and literary meter that is primarily designed for a musical performance (ibid.: xiii). The text is written in the Sindhi (Arabic) script, although the literary work incorporates words and etymological references from a variety of local languages. The literary composition of the text is one of the major indications of the travels undertaken by Bhitai. Additionally, the thematic arrangement of the thirty-six *surs*, derived from specific stories and detailed experiences of a variety of labouring and artisanal communities located across the South Asian region, is another indication of the *Risalo* being a multilayered text. It can be read as a Sufi treatise, a travelogue or as an ethnomusicological text. For more details on the *Risalo*, see Shackle, ed. and trans. (2018).

[5] These are based on the fieldwork I conducted for the Re-centring AfroAsia project between 2018 and 2020. Particularly, I draw from interviews conducted with Mazhar Mutwa, Gani Ustad and Mitho Khan, which are currently in the process of being transcribed for my doctoral thesis.

[6] I refer to all the musicians, *bhagats*, *ustads* that I recorded and interviewed during my fieldwork in 2018. For further reference purposes all the collected material will eventually be made available as part of the RAA repository.

REFERENCES

Ahmed, S. (2004), *The Cultural Politics of Emotion*, New York: Routledge.

Gallagher, S. (2013), 'The Socially Extended Mind', *Cognitive Systems Research*, vols 25–26, pp. 4–12.

_____ (2017), 'Theory, Practice and Performance', *Connection Science*, vol. 29, no. 1, pp. 106–18.

Hawley, J.S. (2015), *A Storm of Songs: India and the Idea of the Bhakti Movement*, Cambridge, Mass.: Harvard University Press.

Hawley, J.S., C.L. Novetzke and S. Sharma, eds (2019), *Bhakti and Power Debating India's Religion of the Heart*, Seattle: University of Washington Press.

Ingold, T. (2011a), 'Building Living Dwelling: How Animals and People Make Themselves at Home in the World', in *The Perception of the Environment: Essays on Livelihood, Dwelling and Skill*, London and New York: Routledge, pp. 172–88.

—— (2011b), 'Maps, Wayfinding and Navigation', in *The Perception of the Environment: Essays on Livelihood, Dwelling and Skill*, London and New York: Routledge, pp. 219–42.

Shackle, C., ed. and trans. (2018), *Shah Abdul Latif Risalo*, Cambridge, Mass.: Harvard University Press.

Sharma, D. and F. Tygstrup, eds (2015), *Structures of Feeling: Affectivity and the Study of Culture*, Berlin: De Gruyter.

Taylor, D. (2003), *The Archive and the Repertoire*, Durham: Duke University Press.

Williams, R. (1977), *Structures of Feeling: Marxism and Literature*, Oxford: Oxford University Press.

3

From *Qaul* to *Haul* or Vice Versa

Musical Circulation between Western Sahara and India from Twelfth to Fifteenth Century

LUIS GIMENEZ AMOROS

The circulation of certain musical expressions across a vast inter-connected world from India to al-Andalus reveals the cultural interaction between three continents before the advent of the colonial era. Since 2004 the author has been exploring musical expressions that reveal such historical interconnectedness, specifically between pre-colonial Spain (Gimenez Amoros 2018a), Africa (Gimenez Amoros 2015, 2018b), the Arabic Gulf and India.

Before gaining insight into musical circulation from Western Sahara to India, it is crucial to reconsider the pre-colonial mobility of music prior to the divide between western and non-western knowledges by colonial tropes. It is evident that the notion of non-western knowledge arises from the genesis of the colonial project as a form of global domination that developed and exists till the present day, producing its own jargon – the Other, exotic, primitive, Oriental, non-civilized, etc. Further, the colonial project and its series of historical periods – the Middle Ages, Renaissance, Baroque, Classical, Romantic, Contemporary, Modern, Postmodern – do not always address the crucial relationship between the so-called 'west' and the expansion of the Islamic world for the development of music since the revival of Greek philosophy in the ninth century. This historical relationship is clearly evidenced by Charlemagne's (the

Roman emperor during the ninth century) interest in the cultural heritage of Islamic culture:

> Charlemagne tried to emulate and compete with Baghdad and Cordoba. He too invited scholars from abroad to his court and established schools. This revival was chiefly mastered by three influential scholars: Theodolfus (d. 821), Claudius (d. *c.* 839) and Agobardus (d. 840), all of whom had contacts with Muslim learning as they were Goths born or educated in Spain or Southern France. In addition to his friendship with the Abbassid Caliph, Harun Al-Rashid, the renowned Chanson de Geste revealed that Charlemagne spent seven years in Spain. (Saoud 2004: 7)

In order to understand one of the key questions of this article about the musical circulation between Western Sahara and India, the *haul* modal system – which applies to poetic and musical forms of composing songs in five northern countries in North Africa, although historically popularized in present Mauritania – is related to other musical and poetic forms of composing songs, such as the *noubat* in Andalusi music (still performed in Algeria, Morocco, Tunisia and Libya); the *maqāmat* under the cultural influence of the Ottoman Empire such as in Egypt, Turkey or Iraq; Persian singing; the Greek modes; and *qawwali*/Hindustani rāgas among other interconnected musical styles. The musical commonalities between Western Sahara and India reflect an interconnected cultural world of 'creating and borrowing'.

In addition to the relevant musicological and performative aspects of interaction in the music, this article also addresses the interdisciplinarity of music during the pre-colonial period where the study of music is related to philosophy, mathematics and geometry among other disciplines. Particularly from the ninth century onwards, there is an 'Islamic Renaissance period' in which Islamic scholars from various geographical areas (Iran, Spain, Iraq, Syria) study music in an interdisciplinary and inter-religious form by including and revitalizing ancient Greek philosophy of music.

Specifically, from the ninth to the eleventh century, there are significant contributions to the study of music such as al-Kindi's (870 CE) on the mystic knowledge of music, that of his disciple al-Farabi who wrote *Kita al-Musiqa al-Kabir* ('the great book of music') where he studies the musical intervals between notes or the pre-Islamic influence of Khorasani music in Syria (Ranade 2008: 15). One of the most significant contributions to the study of the interdisciplinarity of music during the pre-colonial period is the book entitled *Music, Sound, and Architecture in Islam* (Frishkopf and Spinetti, eds 2018), which reveals the correlation between music, mathematics, geometry or architecture from Spain to India. As part of the inter-disciplinarity of music during the ninth century, one can add the medicinal aspect of music mentioned by many music theorists from that century onwards.

Hence, *maqāms* were formed theoretically first by al-Kindi (801–873 CE) and al-Farabi (870–950 CE) in the same century; then İbn-i Sina (980–1037 CE) studied al-Farabi's *maqām* theory in the tenth and eleventh centuries in his book called *Kitabü'ş-şifâ* ('book of healing'), but he used *maqām* music generally for the treatment of patients (Yöre 2012: 267).

With regard to the borrowing of Hindustani and *qawwali* music as a result of the cultural circulation across a vast interconnected world, Ranade (2008: 9) states that the creation of Hindustani/ *qawwali* music is based on a 'performative exchange' that 'does not begin, continue and end somehow'. In his notion of 'performative exchange', he also asserts that 'the most important and inevitable achievement of cultural zones is of course the circulation of ideas, processes, and objects' (ibid: 11). In other words, the notion denotes the circulation of intangible ideas (music, philosophy, etc.) through tangible musical instruments. For Ranade, the cultural zone where *qawwali* and Hindustani music originates would include ancient Greece, the Arab world, Persia and India. Thus, like the author, Ranade addresses certain cultural relationships that appeared in the pre-colonial world, such as the possible link between *haul* and *qaul*.

In doing so, he expresses his concern about analysing the circulation of music without becoming centralized in one specific area of research, thus becoming Indo-centric or 'somewhere else centric'. He notes that 'the only excuse is my personal incapacity to exhaustively explore the multiple, connected and wider areas' (ibid: 12). In accordance with Ranade acknowledging the personal limitations of studying such cultural circulation, while this article demonstrates a certain interconnectivity between Western Sahara and India, due to my own limitations, I will focus on a comparative study with a clear emphasis on Western Saharawi music and its commonalities across the Sahara, sub-Saharan Africa and the Indian Ocean.

The pre-colonial territory where the Hassani people from Yemen migrated covers the whole of Mauritania and Western Sahara, and, in addition, a small portion of southern Morocco, southwestern Algeria and northeastern Mali.

Norris (1962) gives an account of the migration of the Yemeni communities of Ibn Halal and Ibn Hassan to Trab el Bidan, a pre-colonial territory related to the linguistic area where Hassanya is spoken (the main national language in Mauritania and Western Sahara). R.B. Serjeant, himself a specialist in southern Arabia, was also struck by the cultural similarities after he had seen our expedition film of life in the caravan towns of Chinguetti and Wadan. There appears to be a clear case for some cultural contact, but having postulated this, it is extremely difficult to tabulate or classify it. This cultural contact does not concern Mauritania alone but includes those vast areas of the Sahara and the Sudan, to the east and the south, which lie astride the routes leading to the Arabian Peninsula (ibid).

There were two commercial routes through which Africa (Sahara and sub-Saharan Africa) and the Arabic Gulf were interconnected after the Yemenite communities settled in Trab el Bidan: the desert route from Western Sahara towards Sudan and the Arabic Gulf; and the coastal route from Mauritania through Spain and North Africa. According to Saharawi sources, some of the trading goods were ostrich feathers and marble or gold dust from Sudan.[1] It is evident that the connection of the Hassani people with the Arabian Peninsula was partly due to the pilgrimage to Mecca, one of the main foundations for the interconnectedness between Africa, the Arabic Gulf and Asia.[2] One of the possible cross-cultural influences between *haul* and *qawwali* relates to the meeting point with Yemen–India (through the Hajj route to Mecca and by sending mercenaries from Yemen to different parts of present-day Pakistan and Gujarat since the sixteenth century) and Yemen–Trab el Bidan (by Yemenites migrating to Western Sahara or by their pilgrimage to Mecca from Western Sahara). The third possibility of cultural interaction between India and Western Sahara relies on the connection by Saharawi-Berbers with al-Andalus through the revival of Greek philosophy since the ninth century.

In Trab el Bidan, the *haul* modal system originated with the construction of the Hassani identity gradually formed with the coexistence of Yemenite people and Berbers. The Berber Sanhaya had lived in most parts of Trab el Bidan since the third century. During the seventh century, the Berber empire expanded from Spain to Ghana through different Berber communities. Sanhaya, the predominant Berber community in Western Sahara, were mostly Christians or Jewish (Rodriguez Esteban, ed. 2011: 16). Therefore, the Islamization of Trab el Bidan – including the introduction of the *sunna* based on the *Maliqui* school – was not completed until the arrival of the Yemenite Arabs during the fourteenth and fifteenth centuries, thereby forming a geographical region known as Trab el Bidan (Gerteiny 1967: 28).

The coexistence of the Banu Hassan branch with the Berber Sanhaya created the Hassanya language. Hassanya is an Arabic dialect, around 80 per cent of which is based on classical Arabic combined with Berber words. In addition, the encounter between Yemenite Arabs and Berbers created a type of hierarchical society known as the Hassani (Rodriguez Esteban, ed. 2011: 17). According to Cleaveland (1998: 367), the social structure of the Hassani was based on a stratified society divided into four different levels:[3]

Level 1: *Chorfa* (direct descendants of the Prophet), at the top of the pyramid. They were the Arab Yemenite communities Banu Hassan and Banu Hilal.

Level 2: *Arab* (warriors) and *zuaia*, who were people dedicated to religious studies and meditation.

Level 3: Pastoralists, farmers, fishermen and Berber descendants. They had to pay taxes to the higher classes.

Level 4: Black slaves, *igagwen* (musician castes), blacksmiths and Berber-Jewish or Christian descendants.

At level 4, next to the sub-Saharan slaves, blacksmiths and Jewish or Christian descendants, *igagwen* (musician castes) were in the lowest rank of the Hassani social structure. In ancient Hassanya society, it was believed that music was inherited through genes and so *igagwen* families possessed the art of music, and it was believed that music passed from one generation to the next in every *igagwen* family.

A similar concept to *igagwen* is the term *jeli* (or *griot*).[4] Durán (1999: 542) notes that *jelis* 'entertained the nobility with their epic songs and stories about the major events in Mande history'. He refers to the *jelis* as the keepers of history and epic stories occurring in some local kingdoms (Mansa) in the Mande empire in West Africa (ibid.). However, such a concept of *jeli* as a reporter and oral historian is more related to the Mande empire (mostly in Mali, Senegal, Burkina Faso, Guinea and Gambia) than to the *igagwen* in Trab el Bidan. In the Hassani society, the *igagwen* were only musicians. The responsibility of preserving the oral history through music was conceded to the *chorfa* (level 1) or *zuaia* (level 2), who were poets dedicated to the study of the Koran and Hassanya history. Thus, in the Hassani society, there were social structures of communication among the musicians (level 4) and the poets (levels 1 and 2). This type of artistic relationship between poets and musicians prevails in present-day Mauritania and Western Sahara.

The social engagement between musicians and poets became a

form of cultural and musical interaction for the Hassani society. Therefore, the common role of the *igagwen* and the *jelis* was to entertain and to preserve historical memory in its social context, but with the qualification that the *igagwen* needed a poet to recite poetry based on Islamic principles.

The notion of a musicians' caste also relates to the development of *qaul* by *mirasi* families in northern India and Pakistan. According to Lybarger (2011), the *mirasi* caste recites family genealogies by heart and generally performs at weddings, circumcision and other popular gatherings. In addition, *mirasi* families were also employed in gurdwaras to perform Sikh religious music (ibid.: 106). In comparison to musicians' castes in Mali or Mauritania, *mirasi* families include an inter-religious element in the notion of musicianship in India and Pakistan.

The belief that the musician is not the creator of the poem remains a clear common feature between *mirasi* and the *igagwen* families. However, *qawwali* is sung by the community unlike the *haul* modal system that was first destined to be performed by the *igagwen* to high-caste families. This fundamental difference in the approach to music provides a different form of societal inter-relationship between *haul* and *qaul*.

On the other hand, prior the hierarchical relationship between musicians' castes and higher-class communities in Trab el Bidan, according to different Saharawi sources (Ahmed Fadel, Saharawi historian, interviewed 2 November 2004; Salma and Bara, Saharawi singers, interviewed 6 November 2004), the *haul* originated with the creation of *medej* – an intimate musical style sung to the Prophet since the twelfth century in Trab el Bidan. The devotional and religious approach to the construction of songs to the Prophet (and Sufi saints) through *medej* and *qawwali* remains a fundamental pillar for the development of both the musical styles. Further, the creation of devotional music during the expansion of Islam is closely related to the *tajweed* – a fixed form of reciting the Koran – in conjunction with local influences on composing songs. As a case in point, for centuries, African Muslims have gone to Al-Hazhe University in Cairo to receive professional training in the recitation of the Koran (Scott 2001: 156–58).

DEVOTIONAL AND INTIMATE CONNECTIVITY
BETWEEN *MEDEJ* AND *QAUL*

In Hassani societies, due to their nomadic nature, initiation into Islam differed from that in the rest of the Arab world. They have a philosophical and theological school called *mahadara* (El Hamel 1999: 66). The only condition for admission as a student to the *mahadara* is to memorize the Koran and to have some basic Islamic knowledge, acquired either in elementary school or through family contact. The *mahadara* offers subjects such as the *hadith, fiqh* (Islamic jurisprudence), history, ethics, language, literature, grammar, algebra and theology. This type of religion-based education was prominent in Hassani societies until the beginning of the twentieth century when western education made its appearance (Gerteiny 1967: 62).

According to Ahmed Fadel (interviewed 2 November 2004), from the *mahadara*s and the religious beliefs of Hassani people, Saharawi religious songs known collectively as *medej* were born. As Fadel affirms, in Trab el Bidan, the *mahadara* was the basis of Hassani communities and had its own style of religious songs called *medej*. Although there is no historical evidence of how *medej* originated at the *mahadara*, Koranic knowledge from the *mahadara* was essential to create a religious musical style.

Medej are religious songs that Hassani families sing on a Thursday evening before the sacred day, *al Jummah* (Friday). According to Salma and Bara, in the past, *medej* were a personal way of singing to God. Further, Ahmed Fadel asserts that a *medej* singer could not sing if not inspired. In other words, a *medej* singer could not sing a religious song without creating an atmosphere whereby he/ she felt comfortable singing to God (Ahmed Fadel, interviewed 2 November 2004).

For Salma (interviewed 4 November 2004), *medej* originated after the Prophet's death, and four of his disciples spread *medej* during the expansion of Islam. These four disciples were Abubacar Ebnu Sadik, Ebnu Khattab Omar, Osman and Ali Ebnu Afan Ebnu Ebi Talib (married to the daughter of Muhammad) (Salma and Bara, interviewed 6 November 2004).[5]

Medej and *qawwali* resonate with the notion of *sama*, in which music aims to reach a spiritual state for meditative purposes or 'to nourish the soul' in contact with the creator and Sufi saints (Zuberi 2010: 122). Although a *qaul* generally sings to saints or poems from historical poets like Khusro or Rumi, the poetry in *medej* is mostly devoted to the Prophet or passages from the Koran:

> Hassanya poetry was based on the *Sunna* as the only acceptable way of life among all classes of the Saharan community. The main Sufi orders in Western Sahara were Abdullah Yasin during the fifteenth and sixteenth century in Sagui al Hamra (north of Western Sahara), then the Imam Nasir al-Din in Mauritania in the seventeenth century, and lastly Shaykh Ma al-Aynayn of Smara in the twentieth century. (Norris 1968: 113)

The *Haul* Modal System and Its Musical Interconnectedness with the Desert Trading Route, Middle Eastern *Maqāmat* and Persian *Dastagh*

Haul is a musical system which consists of eight modes and innumerable ways of writing poetry in each mode. One of the first academic references to the *haul* modes is by Nikiprowetzky (1962: 54), who says that Mauritanian scholars are content to define four different modes: (1) *kar* (similar to *seinicar*), for joy and for religious purposes; (2) *fagu*, provoking anger; (3) *signim* (similar to *lyen*), for exciting sensibility; (4) *beigi* (similar to *sgaller*), for bringing sadness. Each mode or *bohr* (literally, 'sea') has its own significance in poetic and musical terms. For instance, *fagu* is a mode that expresses epic stories mostly related to war between different communities. The mode *lyen* is related to love songs; and the mode *sgaller* is related to nostalgic feelings.

The eight melodic modes in the *haul* modal system are *entamas, seinicar, fagu, sgaller, leboer, lyen, lebteit* and *chawada* (or *leharar*).

1. *Entamas*

2. *Seinicar*

3. *Fagu*

4. *Sgaller*

5. *Leboer*

6. *Lyen*

7. *Lebteit*

8. *Chawada or Leharar*

With regard to the commonalities with other musical styles across the desert trading route previously mentioned, the author and Saharawi singer and lyricist Mariem Hassan have composed songs in the *haul* modal systems fused with similar scales from the African continent, such as the *lyen/wassoulou* (Mali) major pentatonic scale in the song 'Arfa'; the use of the mode *chawada* in the song 'Rahy el Aaiun egdat'; or the use of the Dorian pentatonic (or *seinicar*) approximating to the sound of Tuareg bands like Tinariwen in the song 'Addumua'.

There are other *haul* modes closely linked to other musical cultures, such as the similarity between the *sgaller* and *jeli* music from Mali. Outside sub-Saharan Africa, there are clear commonalities between the *haul* modal system, the *maqāmat* modes (*maqām rast/ seinicar, ajam/sgaller* and *hijaz kar/entamas*) or the Persian *dastagh* (*mahur/sgaller, esfahan/fagu* and *bayat e-tork/seinicar*). Similarly, the *hijaz* and *esfahan* mode also appears in the Andalusi *nouba*.

In relation to the development of scales in *qawwali* and Hindustani music, Ranade (2008: 13) mentions that Ibn Misjah (715 CE) provided eight basic melodic frameworks known as *asbi* and probably related to the eight Greek modes. As a case in point, Yöre (2012: 269) notes that 'al-Kindi and al-Farabi based the first *maqām* music theory on Greek music theory'. Thus, the relationship between Greek, Persian and Hindustani music is interconnected from the revival of Greek philosophy up to the standardization of modal systems, namely *maqām*, rāgas or *dastagh*, in the twelfth–thirteenth century.

Ibn Sinna (d. 1037) mentioned some of the existing names of the Persian modal system, such as *nava* or *ispahan* scales (ibid.: 15).[6] The notion of scale arising from the Persian and Greek coexistence influenced the musical systems of a large part of the Asian continent including the *haul* modal system:

> The maqam and raga represent a unique form of the traditional classi-
> cal music of East and both have similar functions. The term *maqam*
> (from Arabic: place, staying) means a musical mode, musical tone, the

position of a tone on musical instrument, or a musical composition. At present *maqam* phenomenon is widely cultivated in vast area including the countries of North Africa (*maqam, nuba*), the near East (in Turkey called *makam*, in Azerbaijan *mugam*, in Iran *dastgah*) and Central Asia (in Uzbekistan and Tadjikistan Shashmaqom, *mukam* in Western China, in Kashmir, *makam* or *Sufiyana kalam*). From thirteenth to sixteenth century phenomenon of maqam (before it was named *pardah*) has a universal system [in all the regions mentioned] named 12 maqams. (Karomat 2006: 62)

Karomat continues by saying that the influence of the Persian *dastagh* and the later notion of *maqāmat* only arrived in India during the eleventh century, although the birth of the *qawwali*'s scales is related to Amir Khusro in the thirteenth century.

From the 11th century A.D., the influence of the Arabic, Persian and Turkic cultures started to fortify its position in North India, and resulted, in particular, in a creation of new genres in Indian literature, art, and music. However, the first important fruits of the assimilation were gained during the Delhi Sultanate in the 13th century and reached the peak later in the 16th–18th centuries during the Great Mughals (Baburids). (Ibid.)

Yöre (2012) also mentions that the notion of *maqām* was systematically classified in Turkey during the thirteenth and fourteenth centuries. We can see that Safiyü'd-Din Urmevî (1224–1294) in the thirteenth century, as well as Selahaddin es-Safedî (1296–1363) and Abdulkadir Merâgî (1353–1435) in the fourteenth century, have systematically classified the *maqām*s which had been made before them in their books (ibid.: 267).

According to Qureshi (1986: 49), the most favoured Hindustani rāgas in *qawwali* are Kafi, Shahana, Bahar, Bageshri and Jaijaivanti. On the other hand, Qureshi notes, the tonal inventory is based on the Bilaval (major scale), Khamaj (mixolydian), Kafi (Dorian) and Kalyan (Lydian) rāgas. In relation to the possible existing rāgas at the beginning of *qawwali*, other scholars have mentioned the main influence of the Persian twelve scales, in which I mentioned the similarities between *mahur/sgaller, esfahan/fagu* and *bayat e-tork/seinicar*.

The earliest evidence of *qawwali*/Hindustani modes that I found were from Ranade's source (2008: 32) in 1556–1605 by Pundaarik Vitthal who listed sixteen rāgas as Persian, such as: Rahayi, Nisavar, Mahura, Jangula, Mahang, Vara, Sunhath, Iraya, Husaeni, Yaman, Sarparada, Vakreja, Hejejika and Musak. According to Karomat (2006), 'Raga Husaini' would have a direct relationship with the construction of Hindustani rāgas at a later stage which derived from the Persian twelve *maqāms*. As a case in point, in 1620, Vyankatmakhi mentions 'Persian rāgas' such as Hussaini (Ranade 2008: 32), which is a mode found in Andalusi music. However, with regard to the commonalities between the *haul* modal system and *qawwali*, I only found commonalities between Kalyan (Lidyan) and *sgaller*. These modes are also connected to the Andalusian mode *raml al-máya*.

CONCLUSION

The possibilities of interconnectedness between *haul* and *qaul* reveal a cultural circulation through the expansion of Islam; its revival of Greek philosophy from the ninth century onwards by revitalizing the interdisciplinarity of music, philosophy and the sciences; and the consequent flourishing of musical modes (beyond the eight Greek modes) and ways of writing poetry. Further, the birth of devotional songs in Sufi music portrays a Muslim world influenced by pre-Islamic and local musical forms such as the sub-Saharan influence of *haul* instruments or the different languages and musical influences used in *qawwali*. This paper aims to demonstrate that the circulation of musical knowledge had certain commonalities, such as the song structure, the musical relationship with religious and devotional poetry or the 'way of performing various instruments' during the Islamic expansion.

NOTES

[1] Retrieved from http://www.umdraiga.com/rasd/CapituloII.htm on 12 February 2018.

[2] In relation to the connection between India and Yemen through pilgrimage routes, as the possible meeting point between the Hassani and *qawwali*, the historical Hajj route connected Syrian, Iraqi and Indian Muslims on their transoceanic route to Mecca through the Yemenite town Aden (Petersen 1994). Further, Yemen exported soldiers to India among whom many settled in India, such as the Jamaatis who guarded the Hyderabad Nizams or previously the soldiers that defended the sultan of Gujarat in the sixteenth century.

[3] *Qawwali* music too developed in a hierarchical society divided into four levels – brahmans (priests), kshatriyas (rulers), vaishyas (farmers, traders), sudras (servants) – which may reveal a connection between these two societies.

[4] 'The *griot* culture extends throughout northwest Africa. It is understood as a musical caste in the regions of the Mande empire and in Trab el Bidan. The main indigenous theory about *griots* is that music is genetically inherited within family castes. Thus, the musician has a certain surname dating back to the time of the local kingdoms' (Gimenez Amoros 2012: 21).

[5] According to Bhattacharjee and Alam (2012), 'The propagation of Sufism started from its origin in Baghdad, Iraq, and spread to Persia, Pakistan, North Africa, Central Asia and Muslim Spain. Sufism has produced a large body of poetry in Arabic, Turkish, Persian, Kurdish, Urdu, Punjabi, Sindhi and even Bangla, from which the genre of Sufi music, lyrics and qawwali has emerged.' Particularly, Bhattacharjee and Alam trace back to the eighth century the birth of Sufism in a new educational system 'set up by the Baghdadi Caliphate state provided for the setting up of seminaries of higher learning (called madrasas) where scholars were taught how to run the government in accordance with orthodox Sunni ideas. These scholars were known as ulema and they wielded political power and influence in the Islamic states, including medieval India.'

[6] Prior to the revival of Greek philosophy in Persia, '[t]he Greco-Iranian musical exchanges have enjoyed a long tradition as mentioned by Herodotus (500 BC), Xenophen (550 BC) although after Alexander the Great invaded Iran in 334 BC, he mentioned that the barbat (lute) and the tambur (pandore) inspired Greek instruments such as barbiton and pandoura' (Ranade 2008: 20).

BIBLIOGRAPHY

Bhattacharjee, A. and S. Alam (2012), 'The Origin and Journey of Qawwali: From Sacred Ritual to Entertainment?', *Journal of Creative Communications*, vol. 7, no. 3, pp. 209–25.

Charry, E. (1996), 'Plucked Lutes in West Africa: An Historical Overview', *The Galpin Society Journal*, vol. 49, pp. 3–37.

_____ (2000), *Mande Music*, Chicago: University of Chicago Press.

Cleaveland, T. (1998), 'Islam and the Construction of Social Identity in the Nineteenth-Century Sahara', *The Journal of African History*, vol. 39, no. 3, pp. 365–68.

De la Courbe, S. (1913), *Premier Voyage du Sieur de la Courbe Fait a la Coste d'Afrique en 1685*, Paris: Palais Culturel.

Durán, L. (1995), 'Birds of Wasulu: The Freedom of Expression and Expression of Freedom in the Popular Music of Southern Mali', *British Journal of Ethnomusicology*, vol. 4, no. 1, pp. 101–34.

_____ (1999), 'Mali', in S. Broughton, M. Ellingham and R. Trillo, eds, *World Music: Africa, Europe and the Middle East*, vol. 1, London: The Rough Guides, pp. 539–63.

El Hamel, C. (1999), 'The Transmission of Islamic Knowledge in Moorish Society from the Rise of the Almoravids to the 19th Century', *Journal of Religion in Africa*, vol. 29, no. 1, pp. 62–87.

Frishkopf, M. and F. Spinetti, eds (2018), *Music, Sound, and Architecture in Islam*, Austin: University of Texas Press.

Gerteiny, A.G. (1967), *Mauritania*, London: Pall Mall Press.

Gimenez Amoros, L. (2006), *Los Mares del Desierto*, Villena: Visualsonora.

_____ (2012), 'Haul Music: Transnationalism and Musical Performance in the Saharaui Refugee Camps of Tindouf, Algeria', doctoral dissertation, Rhodes University, Eastern Cape, South Africa.

_____ (2014), 'I Play Wassoulou, Jeli, Songhay and Tuareg Music: Adama Drame in Postcolonial Mali, Bimusical or Multimusical?', *El Oído Pensante*, vol. 2, no. 2, pp. 1–14.

_____ (2015), 'Transnational Habitus: Mariem Hassan as the Transcultural Representation of the Relationship between Saharaui Music and Nubenegra Records', doctoral dissertation, Rhodes University, Eastern Cape, South Africa.

_____ (2018a), 'Un Enfoque Etnomusicológico del Orientalismo: El Estudio Musical e Histórico de las Fiestas de Moros y Cristianos en Villena (España)', *El Oído Pensante*, vol. 6, no. 1, pp. 54–72.

_____ (2018b), *Tracing the Mbira Sound Archive in Zimbabwe*, New York: Routledge.

Hart, D.M. (1962), 'The Social Structure of the Rgibat Bedouins of the Western Sahara', *Middle East Journal*, vol. 16, no. 4, pp. 515–27.

Karomat, D. (2006), 'The 12-Maqam System and its Similarity with Indian Ragas (according to Indian Manuscripts)', *Journal of the Indian Musicological Society*, vol. 36, no. 62–71.

Khan, S.E., A.G. Chaudhry, H. Farooq and A. Ahmed (2015), 'Reviewing Qawwali: Origin, Evolution and its Dimensions', *Science International*, vol. 27, no. 2, pp. 1701–04.

Lybarger, L.H. (2011), 'Hereditary Musician Groups of Pakistani Punjab', *Journal of Punjab Studies*, vol. 18, nos 1 and 2, pp. 97–130.

Mercer, J. (1976), *Spanish Sahara*, London: Allen and Unwin.

Nikiprowetzky, T. (1962), 'The Music of Mauritania', *Journal of the International Folk Music*, vol. 14, pp. 53–55.

Norris, H. (1962), 'Yemenis in the Western Sahara', *The Journal of African History*, vol. 3, no. 2, pp. 317–22.

—— (1968), 'Shaykh Ma´al-Aynayn al-Qalqami in the Folk Literature of the Spanish Sahara', *Bulletin of the School of Oriental and African Studies*, vol. 31, no. 1, pp. 113–36.

—— (1971), 'New Evidence on the Life of Abdula B. Yasin and the Origins of the Almoravid Movement', *The Journal of African History*, vol. 12, no. 2, pp. 255–68.

Petersen, A. (1994), 'The Archaeology of the Syrian and Iraqi Hajj Routes', *World Archaeology*, vol. 26, pp. 47–56.

Qureshi, R. (1986), *Sufi Music of India and Pakistan: Sound, Context and Meaning in Qawwali*, Oxford: Oxford University Press.

Ranade, A.D. (2008), *Perspectives on Music: Ideas and Theories*, Delhi: Promilla Publishers.

Rodriguez Esteban, Jose A., ed. (2011), *España en Africa: La Ciencia española en el Sahara Occidental, 1884–1976*, Madrid: Calamar Ediciones.

Scott, M. (2001), 'The Muslim Call to Prayer', in V. Danielson, D. Reynolds and S. Marcus, eds, *The Garland Encyclopaedia of World Music*, vol. 6, New York: Routledge, pp. 153–63.

Saoud, R. (2004), 'The Arab Contribution to Music of the Western World', UK: Foundation for Science, Technology and Civilization.

Viitamäki, M. (2009) 'Where Lovers Prostrate: Poetry in the Musical Assemblies of Chishti Sufis', *Studia Orientalia Electronica*, vol. 107, pp. 311–44.

Yöre, S. (2012), 'Maqam in Music as a Concept, Scale and Phenomenon', *Zeitschrift für die Welt der Türken/Journal of World of Turks*, vol. 4, no. 3, pp. 267–86.

Zuberi, I. (2010), 'Jashn-e-Khusrau: A Collection', in S. Hossain and I. Zuberi, *Jashn-e-Khusrau: A Collection*, Delhi: Roli Books, pp. 122–48.

INTERVIEWS

Ahmed Fadel, in *wilaya* of Auserd, Algeria, 2 November 2004.

Ahmed Zein, in *wilaya* of Auserd, Algeria, 2 November 2004.

Salma, in *wilaya* of Auserd, Algeria, 4 November 2004.

Bara, in *wilaya* of Auserd, Algeria, 6 November 2004.

Salma and Bara, in *wilaya* of Auserd, 6 November 2004.

Ali Seibda, in *daira* of Birganduz, Algeria, 13 November 2004.

Lualy Lehsan, Algeria, 19 November 2004.

Mariem Hassan, in Villena (Spain), 1 December 2011 and 1 August 2012.

Baba Jouly, in Madrid, 23 June 2012.

4

The Musical Connections of AfroAsia through the Afro-Spiritual Consciousness of *Ngoma*

NKOSENATHI ERNIE KOELA

THE FLUIDITY OF TIME

The ritualized formation of the concept and consciousness of *ngoma* within African peoples presents itself through a myriad of cultural and ritual formations. In Africa, *ngoma* is a systematized ecology of healing with identifiable markers that makes it distinctly part of its African tradition. The gradual or forced mobilization, globalization and movement of Africans into the old and the new world meant that they brought with them their ideas, knowledge, trade, practices and belief systems. I believe that *ngoma* in India was a technology taken via the Indian Ocean by individuals and groups from the coast and hinterlands of the African continent. The Siddis of Gujarat and other parts of India form a part of the community who have formulated new imaginations to the ritual and spiritual formations of *ngoma* through the embodied practice of music and prayer in India.

The re-centring of Africa and Asia by looking at the period 1000–1500 CE allows for an understanding of the African diaspora, being the 'movements' of people from Africa into the world in a new light. This time frame allows thinkers the space to imagine more, through interdisciplinary research, the older history of Africa and Asia's connections. Simultaneously, it asks various questions such as who these peoples were, what they brought to their relocated spaces – in the form of food, a culture, a musical practice or a language – and what they left behind, allowing for researchers to gauge the differences and/or similarities between the original cultures and current realities.

An appraisal of these changes is extremely important for it gives one a tool to understand the diaspora not only through the lens of slavery or conquest, but also through people, a way of life and a vibrant cross-cultural experience that all lead to and from Africa. It also reaffirms that both Asia and Africa were always a part of a world history constituting a large part of the culture that persists today.

Africans were and are part of the global community in Asia. Africans came over the Indian Ocean as merchants, military personnel and servants (Jayasuriya and Pankhurst, eds 2003). For example, in Makran, a quarter of the total population was of African descent. The exhibition, *The African Diaspora in the Indian Ocean World,* showed that African peoples entered the area known today as Pakistan from Baluchistan and Sindh (Schomburg Center for Research in Black Culture 2011). It is recorded that the ship merchants in that region still sing songs that closely resemble songs of the Swahili coast; the songs make use of Swahili and some adapted Swahili (ibid). Linguists have suggested that particular words used in India by specific groups said to be of African descent are similar or identical to words still used in countries that speak Swahili in Africa (ibid). For example, the word *ngao* in Swahili means 'shield', and for the Afro-Indians called the Siddi, *goa* is the word used for shield (ibid). In Gujarat, Africans were involved in trade and in war as early as the first century CE. Oral traditions described individuals said to be from Ethiopia as major actors in Gujarati history. The Siddis, for example, have accounts of many of their ancestors acting as guards in palaces.

The Siddis are a community in India that has a very important role in connecting the heritages of Africa and Asia today. Scholars have looked at various accounts of the impact that the Siddi community had both locally and globally (Alpers 2004). One such example shows that although some Siddis went as enslaved individuals to India via the Indian Ocean route, this did not necessarily mean that they could not and did not effect change. Thus, the records show that the agate beads that went from Asia to the world were, because of the Siddi Gori Pir, also referred to as Bava Gor (Catlin-Jairazbhoy and Alpers 2004). Gori Pir or Bava Gor was an Abyssinian known for effecting revolutionary changes to the production and exportation of agate beads internally within Asia and externally to the world as far as his ancestors' home in Abyssinia/Ethiopia (Alpers 2004).

AFRICAN, AFRICANNESS: TRADE AND IDENTITY POLITICS IN THE INDIAN OCEAN

Alpers (2004) suggests that Africans were sent through varying trade routes, ruled by different religious, social and ethnic communities. Therefore, how the enslaved were or expected to be treated differed from region to region. For example, in Gujarat many Africans came with the Arab traders through the Persian Gulf, while in Uttara Kannada traders took enslaved Africans through East Africa. The youngest traders were the Portuguese who were said to use mostly the coasts of Zanzibar and Mozambique (ibid.). Each route indicates a time period and had slavers treating the enslaved differently according to their culture, religion, dynamics and the reasons for their slave trade.

Prita Meier argues that Paul Gilroy's 1993 book, *The Black Atlantic*, which focuses on routes and not roots, is a helpful starting point for mapping and understanding identities and connections for Africa and Asia (Meier 2004: 96). Focusing on where peoples were taken to (their route) provided a methodically different point of departure when looking at the construction of identity within the Indian Ocean.

Meier elaborates this argument by saying that this approach can assist in unpacking what constitutes assimilation, acculturation, identity formation, and the political and social nuances and tensions as they exist for the Siddis, who find themselves wedged between India and Africa. I agree that there is difficulty in finding the origins of connections in such a confusing, scarcely researched and complicated history. Adopting Gilroy or Meier's idea of looking at the effects instead of the causes could benefit us more in understanding the positionality and connections we are looking for as expressions related to the past but not always rooted immovably in it. Thus, we can allow for a more fluid understanding of peoples, and their material and non-material cultures.

The Siddis were involved in many ways with the trade history of the Indian Ocean. Their roles within Asia impacted the military, the royal courts and material culture greatly between the tenth and fifteenth centuries. They were sent as human cargo from Ethiopia, also known as Abyssinia, and taken through various trade routes to different empires and sectors in Asia. For example, slave traders took slaves from Abyssinia through Godar, Massawa and Zeila, while other slaves were taken to Cairo through the Ottoman Empire (Omar 2016).

Faruq Bhai, a Siddi I met during my travels to India, described to me the complexities of the positionality that came with being Siddi. Being Siddi meant one was part of a caste, a racial category, a scheduled tribe, *habshi* or *sayid*, poor or cunning, happy or strong, loyal, and much more (personal communication, 2017). Siddi has come to denote many things, one of which is race – i.e. the term identifies those with Afro-looking features – both to Indians and to the Siddis themselves. These denotations are a product of the history of slave routes. For example, the etymology of the word *habshi* comes from its meaning 'Ethiopia' in Arabic. On my visit to India, I encountered Siddis who used the term with a sense of pride and not oppression – perhaps an instance of subversion, I am not sure. Similarly, the etymology of the word Siddi according to Omar (2016: 9) has competing interpretations: on the one hand, he writes, it could be a derivative of the Arabic word *sayd*, meaning 'captive', or, on the other hand, it could be a word that refers to those who are said to be of Prophet Muhammad's lineage.

It is clear, however, that the Siddis were and are in a peculiar position in Asia, because historically they were dehumanized but still eroticized as objects with qualities that made them valuable (Omar 2016). They were, if you will, objects enslaved in some form physically, through servitude or conscription, and therefore objectified. This is why their beauty, strength, bravery, loyalty and other attributes were so desired by the Mughals and the Islamic slave traders.

Alpers, in *Africans in India* (2004: 28) suggested that the number of Africans in India was relatively small for various reasons – one being that India had a large population and labour supply, and therefore did not need to enslave people for purposes of labour, unlike in Iraq where many people from Zanj were imported to work on the land. In the tenth century, Muslim slave traders used African peoples as military slaves to run wars, protection and campaigns (Alpers 2004); others were eunuchs with political and social status and responsibilities. Some were free people, including business people such as Bava Gor; some were skilled in caring for and training horses; while others were even rulers. It is clear that the stories of Africans in the Indian Ocean are myriad and that no one story can capture the range of African experiences. However, the common story of the Siddis is that their ancestors were from Africa and went to Asia at varying points in time, and thus their connection to Africa is in essence their heritage.

Between the thirteenth and the fourteenth centuries the Habshis were tools used for military expansion and campaigns by the Muslim Arab Sultans and Indians alike, who required their skill, bravery and power (ibid). Habshi Siddi Yaqut was an individual who was used in such military exploits to take control of Janjira, which the Siddis ran successfully from the sixteenth to the eighteenth century, only to be thwarted by British invasion and colonization (ibid.).

It is interesting to note how the trans-Atlantic slave trade routes produced individuals who were not even allowed to read books, because their enlightenment posed a threat. Conversely, in the Indian and Arabic slave trade, we find that individuals had access to weapons and other opportunities. The route that individuals took indicated who enslaved them and at what time, and therefore what type of enslavement they were under. This again indicates that if one wants to analyse the type of life and culture an enslaved individual had and may have adapted to, looking at what route they took is a very valuable means. As opposed to a focus on where the individual came from, it can be argued that the routes of origin can give a better insight into the type of life and community that enslaved peoples built.

However, with these types of histories there are complex interconnections, and so, perhaps, looking at both roots and routes can assist in comprehending a culture's material and social dynamics. Inasmuch as the route is designed to strip the enslaved of their roots, some vestiges of the old self do remain; and those we can cite in what remains of their identity of Africanness in foreign climes.

The Portuguese only became slave trade actors in the sixteenth century, and mainly used the coast of Mozambique for trading in materials and people. The task of tracking the numbers and familial and ancestral ties of the descendants of these slaves within India was almost impossible, because, unlike in the trans-Atlantic region, where detailed accounts of persons were maintained, in the Indian Ocean trade, such details were ignored. For example, instead of detailing where an enslaved individual was from, his name and perhaps his family name, the Portuguese log-books wrote down only one name for all the enslaved – Abdulla Mubarak, which means 'servant of god for Abdulla' and 'one who is blessed or kneeling for Mubarak' (Alpers 2004: 20). This makes it difficult to locate the roots and origins of peoples, their ethnicity, and cultural, social, and religious practices.

Furthermore, in Mozambique I came across an oral history given to me by Borges Gove, a lecturer at Modlane University in Maputo, who suggested to me that the first foreign travellers to encounter Mozambique were the Arabs rather than the Portuguese, and that the name Mozambique is derived from the name of one of these travellers, *Muza–al–biqe* (personal communication, 2017). Thus, it is possible that trade did exist before the Portuguese arrived on the Mozambican coast, and if so, these are the types of conversations we can look into to ferret out these connections.

Kenoyer and Bhan (2004) suggest that the ways in which we think of classification is also racialized, and that racial-essentialist classifications may not be the best means to identify persons of African ancestry. Rather, this is the field of DNA studies, which could assist through more empirical means to give a better picture of those who share their DNA with peoples on the African continent. Similarly, perhaps being Siddi is an identity related to routes and not only roots. When looking at routes Kenoyer and Bhan (ibid.) find that those who identify as Siddi live mainly on the coasts of India. Be that as it may, this information supported by studies such as DNA avoids vague assumptions based on notions of racial essentialism (ibid.).

ROOTS THROUGH MUSICALITY AND SPIRITUALITY

The interconnected effects of roots and routes are reflected in how, amongst the varying paths that Africans took to Asia, they found a way to identify each other and build a collective community. Even through enslavement the cultural formation of the Siddis salvaged a collective history, connected by the idea of their Africanness and sustained by their identity as 'Siddi'. Thus, even if their features may vary in the present, because of centuries of admixture and being taken from different origins in Africa (roots) by different slave traders (routes), they still identify as Siddi.

I wish to ultimately investigate the question: if there is indeed a connection between Africa and Asia, shaped or affected by either roots/origins or routes, can looking at the arts or culture give us an insight as to how different routes can meet in the same roots? In other words, can Siddi art and culture also be traced back to Africa, even though their journey to India was different at varying points in time? Perhaps the arts can give more insight into the social and psychological connections that the Afro-Indian community have created? Are there traceable correspondences within these social cultures on the eastern coast of Africa?

The Siddis, for one, were and are very musical – they were known for their *jkirs*, also known as *dhammal*, which are ceremonial events where Siddis celebrate their saints through song, trance and music (Catlin-Jairazbhoy and Alpers 2004). The malunga, their single-stringed, centrally braced musical bow, was said to be an emblem of the Siddis. The Sufis are spiritual leaders who lead ceremonies like *urs* and *dhammal*, which celebrate Siddi saints and in which they could ask such saints in 'trance possession' ceremonies for guidance and healing (Kenoyer and Bhan 2004).

In the *urs* and *dhammal* ceremonies, Siddis use *ngoma* – song, dance, ideas of ancestry, trance and healing that closely resemble many religious practices on the African continent, which employ similar pathologies of divinity and healing. For example, Lorna Marshall's study on *!Kung* life and trance dances in southern Africa looked at how music and healing are used by the *!Kung* people for ceremonies. In these ceremonial acts of healing, medicine men go into trance and heal the community through ideas of a spiritual entity and energy going through the men, evoked by singing, clapping and dancing (Marshall 1969). Making music and dance for the healing ceremony are a big part of *!Kung* life and enjoyment (ibid.). Similarly, in Niger, Erlmann (1982) notes, not only do drums induce trance, as formerly believed, in *boori* ceremonies, but they rely on stringed and other instruments to induce states of consciousness to connect with the divine.

These are examples of why one could reasonably surmise that the Siddis, who practise similar religious expressions, are closer to customs found on the African continent than those in India, or that, at least, they share cultural connections. This is different from how Arabic Muslims, Christians and Hindus practise their faith, and it is thought-provoking that this Siddi trait makes them a target for varying oppressive tendencies by different religious factions. The Siddis say they practise and do Siddi *goma*. The idea of *ngoma* is a practice in Africa and has its roots in the centre of African religious and spiritual institutions. This *ngoma* of African heritage has deep roots in the Siddi ancestry's cultural and religious practices.

Conclusion

The practice of Siddi *goma* marks a unique religious hybridity in the Indian Ocean. The Siddi tangibly intertwine *ngoma* with their existing environment, thereby making it useful for them in their current contexts. This illustrates how fluid and dynamic *ngoma* has been as a cultural-religious technology for Africans both within and outside Africa. It also indicates that a new form of religious integration beyond conquest is possible, whereby we see in *ngoma* a negotiation of space, a finding of place to belong, alongside remaining true to one's roots. Thus, where *ngoma* meets Hinduism, Christianity or Islam, depending on the route the Siddis took, they remain grounded in their African roots through *goma*. Unlike conquests that might have accompanied the dissemination of Islam and Christianity, *ngoma* through the Siddis finds itself present in the Indian ecosystem through Indo–African ancestry.

References

Alpers, E.A. (2004), 'Africans in India and the Wider Context of the Indian Ocean', in A. Catlin-Jairazbhoy and E.A. Alpers, eds, *Sidis and Scholars: Essays on African Indians*, Noida: Rainbow Publishers, pp. 27–41.

Erlmann, V. (1982), 'Trance and Music in the Hausa Boorii Spirit Possession Cult in Niger', *Ethnomusicology*, vol. 26, no. 1, pp. 49–58.

Jayasuriya, S.D.S. and R. Pankhurst, eds (2003), *The African Diaspora in the Indian Ocean*, Trenton, NJ: Africa World Press.

Kenoyer, J.M and K.K. Bhan (2004), 'Sidis and the Agate Bead Industry of the Western India', in A. Catlin-Jairazbhoy and E.A. Alpers, eds, *Sidis and Scholars: Essays on African Indians*, Noida: Rainbow Publishers, pp. 42–61.

Koela, E.N. (2019), '"Seeds of the Braced Bow" (The Flower, the Seed and the Bee)', MA thesis, Faculty of Humanities, College of Music, University of Cape Town, available at https://open.uct.ac.za/items/2705a89f-c718-4282-b62e-bd55c14818a9

Marshall, L. (1969), 'The Medicine Dance of the !Kung Bushmen', *Africa: Journal of the International African Institute*, vol. 39, no. 4, pp. 347–81.

Meier, P.S. (2004), 'Per/forming African Identity: Sidi Communities in the Transitional Moment', in A. Catlin-Jairazbhoy and E.A. Alpers, eds, *Sidis and Scholars: Essays on African Indians*, Noida: Rainbow Publishers, pp. 86–99.

Omar, H. Ali (2016), *Malik Ambar: Power and Slavery Across the Indian Ocean*, New York: Oxford University Press.

The Schomburg Center for Research in Black Culture (2011), 'South Asia', in *The African Diaspora in the Indian Ocean World*, http://exhibitions.nypl.org/africansindianocean/essay-south-asia.php (website of the exhibition of the same name), accessed 4 April 2016.

5

The Ngoma Lungundu Drum in Venda Littoral Migrations

Ngoma in the AfroAsian and Global Black Diaspora

SAZI DLAMINI

The term *ngoma*[1] conceptually articulates musical repertoires of embodied ritual performance, belief and spirituality of both African and far-flung transoceanic, diasporic subjects. In attributing sources of their long-held spirituality and religious practices to *ngoma* (and *ngoma* links to Africa), contemporary diasporic subjects in Asia, South America, Caribbean and other oceanic islands reinforce contemporary arguments acknowledging a coeval presence of African descendants in the developing world. The basis of such emergent perceptions of living contemporary cultures stand in contestation to the historical prevalence in northern mainstream scholarship of Africa's othering in the human-peopling and modernizing processes of the world.[2]

The grounding, in socially rooted experience, of what is glibly referred to by the term 'music' in its everyday usage, potentiates an understanding of transmission, retention and deployment of musical elements in black diasporic cultures and their host environments. In its common deployment in mainstream musicological reference, the understanding of the term 'music' merely as 'organized sounds' effectively erases significant meanings of musical performance in indigenous processes of its African provenance. African indigenous musical traditions implicate *ngoma* in performative, material and symbolic elements of meaning-making. Within the conceptual rubric of *ngoma* are included overarching practices that embrace embodied spiritual performances of healing, the engendering and dispelling of transcendental states of being. Musical performance is also central to continuities of shared historical memory, to ritual ceremonies of rites of passage in the human life cycle, ritual communal work, and ancestral and divine communication.

Discrete cultural contexts of *ngoma* are mapped in its overarching permeation of ritual musical performance framing expressive spiritual aspects of individual and socialized consciousness of the Africans, and their Asian and further global diaspora. Common African linguistic references to a drum as *ngoma*, including broadly shared concepts about *ngoma* phenomenology, are geographically endemic to central, eastern, south-western and southern Africa. African trans-ethnic references of the term *ngoma* further include song, dance, organological elements and musical performance associated with spiritual, transcendental and divinatory states of being. Ritual and ceremonial elements of spiritual *ngoma* practices invariably conflate musical repertoires, dances and spoken text to accompany states of expressive musical behaviour of individuals and groups.

The conceptual totality of *ngoma* coalesces broad musical performance terrains of African pre-colonial culture, spirituality and religion, as well as adaptive engagement and discursive contestation of the ideological dominance of successive regimes of colonizing powers (Jantzen 1991; Comaroff and Comaroff 1991; Blacking 1973, 1985; Comaroff 1985; Ralushai 1984; Bernardi 1978; Rutsate 2010; Larsen 2014; Pels 1996; Luongo 2012; among others).

The predominance of *ngoma* in central, east and southern Africa is that of a ritual, social performance; its ideological dominance and institutional ubiquity transcend ethnic and regionally bounded identities. Its performative contexts aggregate a variety of embodied musical performances that address etiological conditions suffered by individual or social subjects. The ritual performances are aimed towards the healing of body and spirit, in practices that include singing, speaking, dancing and performance on musical instruments. Invariably, the embodied performances focus on dance as well as spirit possession and transcendental states of consciousness undergone by *ngoma* participants. In this guise, *ngoma* is considered a dominant trope of African religion and healing practice. Thus, *ngoma* is central in musical practices and repertoires addressing diverse healing practices including exorcism, initiation, gendered rites of passage and cultural socialization of discrete and situated African subjectivities, throughout the African subcontinent and its neighbouring islands.

The elements of the *ngoma* ritual process are common,[3] and pervasively frame musical performances of widely occurring ethno-cultural and intra-ethnic practices of healing. In its therapeutic context, the *ngoma* ritual generally proceeds 'with a declarative statement, prayer, or utterance, then moves on to song begun by the one who makes the statement; as the call and song is developed, the surrounding individuals respond with clapping and, soon, singing begins en masse, and then the instruments enter in' (Jantzen 1991: 291). Healing contexts of *ngoma*[4] in central, east and southern Africa include musical performances of exorcism, ritual songs of wellness and ceremonies for gendered rites of passage (Jantzen 1991, 1995; Johnston 1990; Fair 1996; Hoesing 2012; Koritschoner 1936; Eastman 1986; among others).

Historically, repertoires of African *ngoma* traditions have provided the ideological basis for resistance, adaptation and protest by cultural subjects against colonial and other suppressive institutional regimes (Gunderson 2013). Contestations of social reproductive power of gendered identities have been asserted in *ngoma* female drumming, *ngoma* song, drum and dance performances of masculinity, and labour protest mobilization (Tracey 1952, 1970; Ranger 1975; Bonner *et al.*, eds 1989; Clegg 1981; Erlmann 1991; Sitas and Brauninger 1989; Qabula 2017; Van Schalkwyk 1994; Meintjes 2004; Gearhart 2005). In Latin America, the most substantial African diasporic population is in the central-south and southern states of Brazil. Here, where *ngoma* was brought by the slaves from west-central (Congo, Angola) and east-southern Africa (chiefly Mozambique), its spirituality has persisted in *ngoma* adaptations that venerate Catholic saints in musical performances called *congado* or *congada*.[5]

NGOMA IN BLACK DIASPORA: SIDDI GOMA/DHAMMAL

The originary cultural influence of Black people in Asia (and elsewhere in the inhabited world) is scientifically acknowledged in the DNA of the first modern humans to inhabit the Asian continent, Southeast Asia, Australasia and Japan islands. Black people have been given credit for creating or influencing some of the 'most important and enduring' Asian high cultures of such documented historical periods.[6]

Present-day research on musical and human movement between Africa and Asia seeks to understand cultural relationships that span several centuries. According to Buzurg ibn Shahriyar's *Livre de Merveilles de l'Inde* ('Book of the Wonders of India'), the earliest transcontinental narratives of encounter date back to beyond 300 BCE. This ancient global entanglement documents 'a long history of flourishing trade, commerce and travel between the African continent and India that goes back to the first century CE, when the Indian Ocean was "the world's busiest commercial thoroughfare"' (Shroff 2013: 18). Diverse commodities of exchange included textiles, ivory, rhinoceros' horn and slaves, alongside voluntary migrations undertaken by Africans to different parts of Asia as merchants, traders, sailors, soldiers, healers and many other professions (ibid.). Even in instances where they were still referred to as 'slaves', Africans achieved the highest rank among Muslim societies in the Middle East, India and Central Asia[7] in the course of the first millennium.

AfroAsian historical records provide several terms – Habshis, Abyssinians, Kafirs and Siddis – by which Africans in India have been referred to throughout the different periods of their presence in India, western Asia and Arabia. The Siddis (or Sidis) are contemporary communities of African descendants in the states of Gujarat, Maharashtra, Karnataka, Telangana (formerly part of Andhra Pradesh) and Goa. The Siddi communities thrive in ancient legendary towns and villages that are remarkable for their architecturally celebrated temples and historical religious traditions. In towns such as Ratanpur in Bilaspur district weekly ceremonies are held for the Siddi saint, Bava Gor.[8] The Siddis' ancestors are known to have been adept sailors,[9] whose domineering of India's north-western coast led to the appointment of their commander by the Mughal emperor to the position of admiral of the Indian Ocean (Rashidi and Von Sertima 2007: 17).

Among the Siddis, religious musical practices known as *goma* (or *dhammal*) acknowledge Bava Gor, also a Sufi mystic healer.[10] Although there are no historical records of Bava Gor's life, his arrival in India from Africa forms the basis of a vibrant Siddi oral history and its embedded religious practices. According to history as retold by contemporary Siddis, he was an Abyssinian military leader on a mission from Africa via Arabia to subdue evil spirits and black magic practitioners in Gujarat. He was helped in this task by his brother Bava Habash and sister Mai Mishra. *Goma/dhammal* performances involving dancing and drumming are an integral part of all rituals honouring Bava Gor and Mai Mishra (Shroff 2013: 18). This conjugation in musical conception of artefact, performative context and its processual elements demonstrates diasporic adaptations of traditional contexts for musical practices and repertoires of the *ngoma* of central, east and southern Africa.

Ngoma Lungundu Drum in Karanga-Venda Southward Migration

Ngoma lungundu[11] is the name of the drum which accompanied the Venda on their journey to the south from their purported origins in the Great Lakes region of Tanzania. In the present-day Venda culture, the ngoma lungundu is closely associated with the 'High God' who, like their ancestors in the Kilimanjaro region, is referred to as Mwali or Mwari.[12] The Venda descendancy from Karanga (Shona) relates their ancestry to the Mbire people, whose lineage were priests in shrines dedicated to Mwari during the rule of the Rozvi dynasty based in Great Zimbabwe. In several Bantu languages, the term *muali* means sower, and the god is essentially attributed with fertility of crops and of women.

Venda historical narratives of migration illustrate the centrality of the ngoma lungundu drum in the continuities of the Karanga-Venda clan leadership and cultural integrity as symbolized in ritual musical performance in various social-ceremonial contexts. The drum, which was reconstructed on the basis of accounts of those who carry tradition in the contemporary Venda community, marked the staging of an important dimension in the contemporary Venda memory map of migration. The community carries narratives of their clan custodianship and the guiding presence of the ngoma lungundu or Mwali/Mwari/God's drum. The reconstruction took place as part of the Re-centring AfroAsia project's activities. It is intriguing to encounter the material image of the drum and to participate, in our scholarly curiosity, in the sacred nature of a shared, resilient cultural memory. The musical performance of song–dance–drum marks the convergence of both public historical knowledge and scholarly enquiry about ngoma, its significance and the suffusing of shared diasporic identities in southern Africa.

Once it was reconstructed, the musical and narrative reception ceremony of the ngoma lungundu drum replica was devised by postgraduate research students of the Re-centring AfroAsia project in collaboration with a Khoi spiritual medium and a Xhosa maternal elder, in address of the Supreme God, in respect of spiritual forebears and nature. The symbolic, material dance-movement, sung and spoken elements ceremonially weave ritual *ngoma* practice symbols with those of far-flung AfroAsian black diasporic prayer to the river-god spirit. As in the Karanga-Venda social reverential greeting '*ndau*', the identity of the water spirit in Bantu *ngoma* is also '*ndau*'. The 'replica' of the ngoma lungundu drum is a result of the sculptor's socialization in oral narratives of the Venda people's historical cultural imaginary. The present-day Venda are descended from Kalanga settlers of the historical Mapungubwe precinct and its surrounding littoral landscape. A short video filmed by Thabo Bopape and Jonathan Brady captures an assemblage involving field scholarship, narratives of shared social memory and spiritual rite performance ceremonially presented as *ukuhlangabeza* (in Zulu, 'to come out to meet'). The proceedings document the drum as a 'symbolic' artefact of the Limpopo (South Africa) sculptor Thomas Kubayi's imaginary of the ngoma lungundu. Venda imaginaries of the ngoma lungundu drum straddle vivid strands of resilient social memory and interweave oral narratives of their historical encounters with the San, Khoi, Lemba Bantu,[13] and subsequently with trekker and Boer descendants. The narratives are inherently of migration, conquest and settlement, and thus necessarily about contestations of power. In ngoma lungundu narratives of the Venda people their Karanga ancestors and clan migrations of conquest and defeat are revealed as a geographically vast continuum of shared ideological beliefs and reverent regard for Mwari, the primal deity and conceptual godhead in conquests.

As an oral text, perhaps conflating multiple oral narratives and certainly contestable interpretations over time and space, the Venda ngoma lungundu legend interweaves imaginary threads of the Karanga-Venda diasporic originary myths and narratives of their southward migration. Taken together, the narratives orally affirm the Venda understanding of the relationship between ngoma lungundu as 'the drum of Mwali, the voice of the Great God, King of Heaven (*Mambo wa Denga*), but also of their ancestor God of the Vhasenzhi and Vhakalanga'. Invariably contested, Venda migration narratives parallel other oral histories in which clan victories and defeats depended on adherence to or flouting of the strict rules regarding appropriate handling and sounding of Mwali's drum. At one point the VhaLemba – often considered as the 'Black Jews of southern Africa' – and VhaNdalamo clans were the only ones among Venda's Kalanga or Vhasenzhi ancestors sanctioned to be custodians and carriers of the ngoma lungundu (Schutte 1978: 113).

CONCLUSION

The persistence of the ngoma lungundu drum narratives in contemporary Karanga-Venda historical memory demonstrates the *ngoma* mapping of cultural, spiritual and religious commonalities across generations of Black diasporic descendants, and their historical connections to particularly central, east and southern Africa.

NOTES

[1] In Bantu languages (spoken over a vast area covering central, eastern and southern Africa), including the widely spoken Swahili, 'ngoma' is the common word denoting any kind of drum or drums. *Ngoma* also refers to all genres of music–song–dance that are (primarily) accompanied by drums or drumming, to the whole context of such events or performances (which may include any kind of festive arrangements), and also to a particular *ngoma's* healing or mystical aspects (Graebner 2019).

[2] The African presence in the Indian Ocean world represents one of the most neglected aspects of the global diaspora of African peoples. Yet very significant numbers of people of African descent today inhabit virtually all the countries of the western Indian Ocean littoral. It is evident, however, that African voices have been actively silenced in this diaspora both by the cultural contexts of their host societies and by the way in which the scholarly production of knowledge has reflected such cultural domination (Alpers 2000: 83).

[3] 'Across the region where *ngoma*-type rituals are located, much of central and southern Africa, and certain areas of equatorial Africa, common characteristics include recruitment of those afflicted by a disease, chronic handicap, or social pathology; an initiation-like therapeutic course of several months or years leading from novice to fully-qualified healer status; a redefinition of the self or social group that has been defined as sick, and subsequently stabilized; an etiology of spirit possession that may occasionally be reflected in overt trance, but is often merely hypothesized and dealt with analytically; the tendency to think of the process of going through affliction and healing as a kind of legitimation for other leadership positions' (Jantzen 1991: 290).

⁴ 'The Ndembu call it *kwimba ngoma*, 'to sing a *ngoma*'. The Venda of the northern Transvaal (Limpopo province) speak of *nyimbo dza dzingoma*, singing a *ngoma*. The Kongo of western Bantu 'drum up' (*sika ngoma*) a major *nkisi* medicine with a song, *nkunga*. In the Nguni-speaking setting in southern Africa, the *isangoma*, divine-healer, is one who (*i-*) does (*sa*) *ngoma*. All of these references identify *ngoma* with a patterned rhythm of words, the use of performance dance, and the invocations or the songs which articulate the affliction and therapeutic rite.

⁵ In Belo Horizonte, capital of Minas Gerais (province of Brazil), the cultural anthropologist Sheila Walker 'visited a Congada community that its members called a Mozambique Kingdom . . . in its chapel were statues of Ethiopian saints Benedict and Ephigenia, and they called their drums *goma*' (Walker 2015: 501).

⁶ Since the first modern humans (*Homo sapiens*) in Asia were of African birth, the African presence in ancient Asia can be demonstrated through the history of the Black populations that have inhabited the Asian land mass within the span of modern humanity (Rashidi 1985: 10, in Rashidi and Van Sertima, eds 1985).

⁷ The most celebrated of all African rulers in India is Malik Ambar. Ambar was brought to India in 1575. Born in Ethiopia, he had been a slave in the Middle East. In India he became a trader, and recruited followers and built an army as his trading made him prosperous. He eventually developed such a strong army that he was able to establish himself as the power behind the throne. He invented highly innovative guerrilla warfare tactics, making him formidable and feared by those who challenged his state. He was a brilliant soldier, diplomat and administrator. He appointed his own African ambassador to the court of Persia. He encouraged manufactures, built canals, mosques and a post office. He supported poets and scholars with pensions from the treasury of the state. Joseph E. Harris' chapter on Ambar (in Rashidi and Van Sertima, eds 1985) is indeed one of the most inspiring in the history of Africans in Asia.

⁸ 'Villagers said that Bava Gor had come to Ratanpur from Abyssinia, now Ethiopia, 800 years ago as an agate merchant. He revolutionized the agate stone industry and also demonstrated his spiritual powers by defeating a demoness who had been tormenting the villagers. A devotion to him developed and a shrine that continues to be tended by Sidis was built in his honour. The veneration of Bava Gor has spread beyond the Sidi community and beyond Ratanpur to Mumbai in Maharashtra, as other Indians – Muslims, Christians, Hindus, Zoroastrians – seek healing and blessings from the African saint' (Walker 2015: 508).

⁹ 'In Maharashtra . . . [a] short distance from the small town of Murud [is] the unconquerable island fort of Janjira, now a national landmark, from which Sidis had controlled maritime traffic on India's Konkani coast for centuries' (Walker 2015: 509).

¹⁰ 'The word *goma*, derived from the Swahili word *ngoma*, means song, dance or drum. Sidis often use the Gujarati word *dhammal* interchangeably with *goma*, as explained by a young Siddi man: "Both *goma* and *dhammal* are the same. *Dhammal* is a Gujarati word, *goma* is a Swahili word – it's the same thing – Bava

Gor *ni Dhammal* (Bava Gor's *dhammal*). *Goma* is also dance and the rhythm is
also *goma*, so if you hear music and someone asks 'What's happening?', we can
say '*goma* is going on', and so the song is also *goma*.'" (Shroff 2013: 22)

[11] 'Originally, the Vhasenzi, the ancestors to the royal Singo clan of the Venda
lived in a city called Matongoni ("the graves"). They had this tremendous drum
which was not to be seen by anybody. It was the drum of Mwali, the voice of
the Great God, King of Heaven (*Mambo wa Denga*), but also of the Ancestor
God of the Vhasenzi and Vhakalanga.' (Excerpt from the ngoma lungundu
narrative as told to A.G. Schutte, author of 'Mwali in Venda: Some Observations
on the Significance of the High God in Venda History', by E. Mudau, a Venda
schoolteacher in the 1930s, and published in *Journal of Religion in Africa*, vol.
9, fasc. 2, 1978, pp. 109–22.)

[12] This conception of the High God *Mwari* as inherited by the Venda, was expanded
upon by A.G. Schutte as follows: 'the giver of rain and his most popular praise
name is Dzivaguru, great pool. In addition, he also has great curative powers.
He has both male and female features. As a male he reveals himself in the name
Sororezhou, "head of the elephant" and as a female, in the pool, the dark recesses
of fertility. He is the father of creation who manifests himself in lightning or in
a shooting star coming from above. He is a personal being beyond and above
ancestral hierarchies and could only be approached through the mediation of
the senior lineage age ancestors (*mhondoro* or *vharudzi*) or through his special
messengers' (Schutte 1978: 110).

[13] '. . . a Bantu tribe scattered amongst the Basuto and Bathonga of *those parts*
[Limpopo Province, South Africa], exactly as the Jews amongst European
nations, a tribe having no chief, keeping with a great pertinacity habits totally
different from those of the masters of the country, living and thriving by means
of industry, moreover bearing strong Semitic characteristics . . . the Balemba or
Malemba are called so by the Bathonga [Tsonga]. The Basuto [Sotho] call them
Balepa' (Junod 1908: 276; emphasis mine).

BIBLIOGRAPHY

Alpers, E.A. (2000), 'Recollecting Africa: Diasporic Memory in the Indian
Ocean World', *African Studies Review*, vol. 43, no. 1, pp. 83–99, https://doi.
org/10.2307/524722

Bernardi, B. (1978), 'Embu Cosmological Tales', *Paideuma*, vol. 24, pp. 179–89,
http://www.jstor.org/stable/40341611

Blacking, J. (1973), *How Musical Is Man? The John Danz Lectures*, Seattle: University
of Washington Press.

—— (1985), 'The Context of Venda Possession Music: Reflections on the Effective-
ness of Symbols', *Yearbook for Traditional Music*, 17, pp. 64–87, https://doi.
org/10.2307/768437

Bonner, P., I. Hofmeyr, D. James and T. Lodge, eds (1989), *Holding Their Ground: Class, Locality and Culture in 19th and 20th century South Africa*, Johannesburg: University of the Witwatersrand Press.

Clegg, J. (1981), 'The Music of Zulu Migrant Workers in Johannesburg', in Carol Muller, ed., *Papers Presented at the Symposium on Ethnomusicology, Music Department, Rhodes University on 10th and 11th October 1980*, Grahamstown: International Library of African Music, Institute of Social and Economic Research.

Comaroff, J. (1985), *Body of Power, Spirit of Resistance: The Culture and History of a South African People*, Chicago: University of Chicago Press.

Comaroff, J. and J.L. Comaroff (1991), *Of Revelation and Revolution*, Chicago: University of Chicago Press.

Eastman, C.M. (1986), 'Nyimbo za Watoto: The Swahili Child's World View', *Ethos*, vol. 14, no. 2, pp. 144–73.

Erlmann, V. (1991), 'Horses in the Race Course: The Domestication of *Ingoma* Dance, 1929–1939', in *African Stars: Studies in Black South African Performance*, Chicago and London: University of Chicago Press.

Fair, L. (1996), 'Identity, Difference, and Dance: Female Initiation in Zanzibar, 1890 to 1930', *Frontiers: A Journal of Women Studies*, vol. 17, no. 3, pp. 146–72, https://doi.org/10.2307/3346884

Gearhart, R. (2005), 'Ngoma Memories: How Ritual Music and Dance Shaped the Northern Kenya Coast', *African Studies Review*, vol. 48, no. 3, pp. 21–47.

Graebner, W. (2019), 'Ngoma', in David Horn and John Shepherd, eds, *The Bloomsbury Encyclopedia of Popular Music of the World*, vol. 12, Genres: Sub-Saharan Africa, pp. 454–55.

Gunderson, F. (2013), 'Expressive Bodies/Controlling Impulses: The Dance Between Official Culture and Musical Resistance in Colonial Western Tanganyika', *Soundings: An Interdisciplinary Journal*, vol. 96, no. 2, pp. 145–69, https://doi.org/10.5325/soundings.96.2.0145

Harris, J.E. (1971), *The African Presence in Asia: Consequences of The East African Slave Trade*, Evanston, Illinois: Northwestern University Press.

_____ (1993), *Global Dimensions of the African Diaspora*, second edition, Washington, D.C.: Howard University Press.

Hoesing, P. (2012), 'Kusamira: Singing Rituals of Wellness in Southern Uganda', *African Music*, vol. 9, no. 2, pp. 94–127.

Jantzen, J.M. (1991), 'Self-Presentation and Common Cultural Structures in Ngoma Rituals of Southern Africa', *Journal of Religion in Africa*, 25 (2), pp. 141–62, https://doi.org/10.2307/1581271

_____ (1992), 'Ngoma: Discourses of Healing in Central and Southern Africa', *Comparative Studies of Health Systems and Medical Care*, Berkeley: University of California Press.

_____ (1995), '"Doing Ngoma": A Dominant Trope in African Religion and Healing', *Journal of Religion in Africa*, vol. 21, no. 4, pp. 290–308.

Jaques, A.A. (1931), 'Notes on the Lemba Tribe of the Northern Transvaal', *Anthropos*, vol. 26, nos 1–2, pp. 245–51.

Johnston, T.F. (1990), 'Shangana-Tsonga Dance: Its Role in Exorcism, Initiation, and the Social Beer-Drink', *Anthropologie (1962–)*, vol. 28, no. 1, pp. 89–99.

Junod, H.A. (1908), 'The Balemba of the Zoutpansberg (Transvaal)', *Folklore*, vol. 19, no. 3, pp. 276–87.

Koritschoner, H. (1936), 'Ngoma Ya Sheitani: An East African Native Treatment for Psychical Disorder', *The Journal of the Royal Anthropological Institute of Great Britain and Ireland*, vol. 66, pp. 209–19.

Larsen, K. (2014), 'Possessing Spirits and Bodily Transformation in Zanzibar: Reflections on Ritual, Performance, and Aesthetics', *Journal of Ritual Studies*, vol. 28, no. 1, pp. 15–29.

Luongo, K. (2012), 'Prophecy, Possession, and Politics: Negotiating the Supernatural in 20th Century Machakos, Kenya', *The International Journal of African Historical Studies*, vol. 45, no. 2, pp. 191–216.

Mapana, K. (2007), 'Changes in Performance Styles: A Case Study of *Muheme*, a Musical Tradition of the Wagogo of Dodoma, Tanzania', *Journal of African Cultural Studies*, vol. 19, no. 1, pp. 81–93.

Meintjes, L. (2004), 'Shoot the Sergeant, Shatter the Mountain: The Production of Masculinity in Zulu Ngoma Song and Dance in Post-Apartheid South Africa', *Ethnomusicology Forum*, vol. 13, no. 2, pp. 173–201.

Pels, P. (1996), 'Kizungu Rhythms: Luguru Christianity as Ngoma', *Journal of Religion in Africa*, vol. 26, no. 2, pp. 163–201.

Qabula, A.T. (2017), *A Working Life: Cruel Beyond Belief*, The Hidden Voices series, South Africa: Jacana Media (Pty) Ltd.

Ralushai, V. (1984), 'The Origin and Social Significance of Malombo', paper presented at the Fifth Symposium on Ethnomusicology, Faculty of Music, University of Cape Town, International Library of African Music, 30 August–1 September, .

Ranger, T.O. (1975), *Dance and Society in Eastern Africa, 1890–1970: The Beni Ngoma*, London: Heinemann Educational Books.

Rashidi, R. and I. Van Sertima, eds (1985), *African Presence in Early Asia*, New Brunswick and Oxford: Transaction Books

Rutsate, J. (2010), '*Mhande* dance in the *Kurova Gova* Ceremony: An Enactment of Karanga Spirituality', *Yearbook for Traditional Music*, vol. 42, 81–99.

Schutte, A.G. (1978), 'Mwali in Venda: Some Observations on the Significance of the High God in Venda History', *Journal of Religion in Africa*, vol. 9, no. 2, pp. 109–22, https://doi.org/10.2307/1581392

Shroff, B. (2013), '"Goma Is Going On": Sidis of Gujarat', *African Arts*, vol. 46, no. 1, pp. 18–25.

Sitas, A. and J. Bräuninger (1989), 'Songs from Bambatha's Children', in *Culture and Working Life*, unpublished Music Recording, SAWCO PC 89.

Tracey, H. (1952), *African Dances of the Witwatersrand Gold Mines*, Johannesburg: African Music Society.

_____ (1970), *Chopi Musicians: Their Music, Poetry, and Instruments*, London: Oxford University Press.

Van Schalkwyk, A. (1994), 'The Voice of Protest: Urban Black Women: Song and Resistance the 1980s', unpublished MMus thesis, University of Natal, Durban.

Walker, S.S. (2015), 'Milestones and Arrows: A Cultural Anthropologist Discovers the Global African Diaspora', *The Journal of African American History*, vol. 100, no. 3, pp. 494–21, https://doi.org/10.5323/jafriamerhist.100.3.0494

Wassing, R.S. (1958), 'Review of H. von Sicard's *Ngoma Lungundu: Eine afrikanische Bundeslade*', *Man*, vol. 58, pp. 84–85.

6

Encounters of Asian and African Imaginaries in Rap in France (1981–2012)

PAROMA GHOSE

Europe, and the extensive legacy that it left in the wake of its multinational colonial empires, has not only (effectively) governed the geopolitical realities of the past few centuries, it has also reverse-engineered the discourse on this past so that the study and general understanding of both history and memory continue to hold Europe at their centre (Bhambra and Holmwood 2021). It has thereby over-ridden the connections and exchanges or encounters that took place between non-European societies before, during and after the age of European empires. This is true as much in academia (Austin 2008; Comaroff and Comaroff 2015) as it is in the everyday lived realities of societies across the globe. The western (Europe and the United States of America) domination of popular culture provided an illusory sense of predetermined history (Seago 2000). Global popular culture seemed to confirm Francis Fukuyama's 'end of history' thesis – appreciation of 'other' cultures could only come in the wake of a sense of exhaustion with the west, as an alternative rather than the norm (Featherstone 1990).

Yet, in the light of the recent drive to decolonize knowledge, this long-unquestioned dominance of all things western is undergoing an interrogation, and a vast number of perspectives and encounters outside the auspices of the west are becoming increasingly apparent

(Frank and Gills, eds 1996). One such encounter is that between African and Asian imaginaries in French rap. This paper will examine encounters (musical, societal and of imaginaries) between Asia and Africa through the lyrical gaze of rappers in France. It looks to investigate the absence of certain 'others' from the larger 'other' that continues to exist socially and societally in France through the lyrics and realities of rappers (and the lack thereof), and how, ultimately, they meet on a shared political plane with a common premise.

In my study, I have used the lyrics of French rap to explore histories of the 'other' in France. The lyrics of rap provide ample and living archives that are an alternative take on the realities of the French past. Unwittingly, French rap has become a hub for those who are in some way marginalized in French society to express their discontent. France (which could be taken as a representation of Europe or, rather, a representation of the concept that is commonly understood as the 'west') is where those of varying migratory backgrounds encounter each other. Defined nationally by a geographic boundary which entails the promise of a particular legal structure and system of rights to all those within it, they strive to push the state to deliver on its promises and dues to those that people its land, and the egalitarian universalism that has been enshrined in the French Constitution since 1789 (Hammou 2020; Niang 2019).

Legally, France considers itself a 'colour blind state' (Bleich 2001). In short, this means that France does not draft or enact policies directly addressing racial or ethnic discrimination; its framework of understanding inequality is shaped instead by a focus on socioeconomic echelons (Hargreaves 2015). While this framework is important, in isolation from other intervening inequalities, it has skewed the manner in which France's society has been studied and understood within France itself (Amiraux and Simon 2006). The theory of a France that holds to its universalist dictum and treats all those within its boundaries as equal in the eyes of the law is a well-propagated national myth (Silverman 2002) that resurfaces at regular intervals, particularly in the months preceding presidential elections. France's strong attachment to its idea of itself, hedged on its constitutional foundation and its historical association with the notion of the rights of man, has made it difficult to gauge with any accuracy the reality of the minority experience in the country. It has also, until recently, impeded academic critiques and explorations of the idea and concept of race in France, and where the universalist model fails (Hammou 2020; Niang 2020). With the advent of young French scholars (who, perhaps, were influenced by the dominance of rap in their youth) who are willing to push the boundaries of what is considered worthy of discussion, this academic taboo is slowly being undone.

Moreover, while the colour-blind nature of the French state has made estimating numbers of racial and ethnic minorities difficult, the notion of 'otherness' that is so apparent in the poignant lyrics of French rap songs (1981–2012) is defined by the much wider conception of what it means to 'be French'. It is ultimately an unarticulated idea that is experientially defined, mostly in the negative, when someone 'failing' this assumed national norm is made to feel unwelcome through experiences that occupy a wide spectrum of discriminatory practices (Ghose 2021). This extends to anyone, including French citizens from the Dominion and Overseas Territories (DOM-TOM) such as Guadeloupe and Martinique (which produce a proportionately large number of French rappers), and those whose names quite 'obviously' delineate an origin (regardless of how far back in history) outside of metropolitan France or, as it is otherwise known, the Hexagon. This collective group of minorities is therefore even harder to label, since it is essentially the result of a common experience of being marginalized rather than a defining racial or ethnic discrimination. Not being French is a malleable and flexible concept that can encapsulate anyone considered by state and/or society to be somehow outside its unuttered imaginary. This 'otherness' is therefore where the African and Asian imaginaries in French rap meet.

In the four lyrical samples given below, there are three recurrent themes to note in particular: first, the pointed lambast of France and/or the west; second, the expression of (severe) discontent with the societal status quo because of a continued experience of discrimination, and, most significantly for this paper, the coalescence of people of diverging origins and/or descent in the form of a united collective whom the rappers are representing.

(1) *L'Occident nous a bousillé, comme il bousille tout c'qu'il touche / Mais* **Arabes et Bantous** *n'étaient pas sur le banc d'touche* ('The west ruined us, just as it ruined everything it touched / But Arabs and Bantus were not on the sidelines') – Ghetto Youss (13OR), 'Pour un peuple, un but, une foi', 2005

(2) *La rime urbaine pour toute une jeunesse ici on rêve tous de partir loin d'la tess /* **Antillais, Africain, Maghrébin** */ Parlons peu et parlons bien* ('Urban rhymes for an entire generation here that dreams of leaving the projects/ghettoes [US term] far behind / Antilleans, Africans, Maghrebians / Let's speak little and speak well' – Different Teep, 'Maintenant ou jamais', 1997

(3) *Devant moi, il y a eu* **Mamadou, Icham, Moustafa, Ricardo, Sékou, Hamidou, Youssoufa** */ Mais pendant tout ce temps, j'ai pas vu mon meilleur ami* **Pierre** ('In front of me, there have been Mamadou, Icham, Moustafa, Ricardo, Sekou, Hamidou, Youssoupha / But in all this time, I've never seen my best friend Pierre' – Ad Hoc'1, 'Immigré malgré lui', 1998

(4) *Car leurs locaux sont envahis par des* **blacks et rebeus** */ et des* **toss,** *et des* **tanges,** *des bus remplis* **d'tchong** ('Because their premises are overrun by Blacks and Arabs / and Portuguese, and gypsies, and buses are filled with East Asians' – Dany Dan, 'Case de départ', 2004

The multicultural nature of this unison captures the inadvertent encounter between African and Asian imaginaries in a very poignant and effective way. In excerpt (3), rap duo Ad Hoc'1 identify, in the first instance, the huge variety of people who have stood in front of them while 'queueing for entry and acceptance' (the predominant metaphor, as much as reality, that drives the song). This is accomplished through a listing of names that are designed to immediately evoke an image of a person associated with them, and the community that he (and in this case, they are all male names) represents or with which he can be associated. In this case, we can discern the representation of a spectrum of different African identities, of Islam, and of Italy (Ricardo). This last reference is particularly interesting and may seem in some ways surprising. It alludes to the large number of European migrants who are also at the receiving end of discriminatory behaviour on the basis of their origins, an aspect that we shall explore further when we examine excerpt (4) below. This agglomerated group, then, goes beyond the notion of race and ethnicity, and even deconstructs the idea of a united 'west'. In the following phrase, this idea is reiterated by underlining that their friend 'Pierre', the generically named metaphorical representative of the French 'norm', is nowhere to be found.

In excerpts (1) and (2), meanwhile, the union of those of Arab and those of African origins does not extend to Asia, but instead, stretches further west to encapsulate those from the French Antilles who, despite being legal citizens of the French nation-state, are nevertheless part of this common experience of discrimination. Excerpt (4) is perhaps the most interesting. Dany Dan uses the concept of a literal locale to delineate all the people who would be contained within this space – those of African, Arab, European and Asian origins – and who would collectively inspire fear in the 'locals'. Yet he does so using tendentious slang to denote each of these separate groups, attempting to speak to the French society in an acidulous language that it uses categorically to ostracize people within it. The use of the slang word 'Toss', a pejorative reference to those of Portuguese origin, is a clear reminder that even those of European descent are not exempted from not conforming to the imagined French norm. Estimates from the Institut National des Etudes Démographiques (INED) in 2018 place Portugal as the country of birth of the third largest group of immigrants in France, after Algeria and Morocco; and this is calculated only on the basis of those who were born outside of France, and says nothing of those who are of extra-French descent or origin (INED 2018). Even the term 'Black', which is the most commonly used of all those that Dany Dan cites and may appear to be the most innocuous, has been deconstructed as a controversial import from the English language in the absence of a French equivalent, a literal mark of the absence of any treatment or understanding of race in France or in French (Niang and Soumahoro 2019). Dany Dan has literally weaponized his words and aimed them back at the society that created them to make his point heard.

This lyrical meeting of African and Asian imaginaries is even more striking when we consider that there were very few recognized (in the musical charts) rappers of Asian origin active in the period of study, 1981–2012, particularly in comparison to the number of rappers of African origin. While rappers form a nationally, ethnically and racially diverse group representative of (though not proportionate to) the migrant population (origin and descent) of France, there are only a handful of rappers of Asian origin or descent. This is striking given France's deep imperial history in French Indochina and subsequent post-colonial migration from the now independent nations of Vietnam, Laos and Cambodia to the metropole. Thus, even within the concept of 'the other', there is a centre and periphery.

Research on those of Asian origin in France, particularly in relation to the cultural sphere, is still limited in comparison to that on those of African or Caribbean origin. This makes it difficult to evaluate the different experiences of migrants and thereby to better understand why there are so few musical representatives of certain minority communities in France. Is it that migrants from Africa and Asia do not always coincide in the same geographical spaces, thus removing the first layer of shared common place and experience? Or perhaps it is that migrants from Asia have found different means of communicating and expressing themselves, making rap a less likely recourse for vocalization of their communities' ills. As far as my research has shown, this is a thematic comparison that is yet to be explored.

Yet another layer in this series of encounters between African and Asian imaginaries begs the question of how exactly these imaginaries are constructed in the first place. Given the proportionately large representation of African countries amongst rappers in France, African imaginaries are often grounded in specific national references (rapper Black M refers to Guinea-Conakry, rapper Youssoupha to the Democratic Republic of Congo, etc.). Where 'Africa' as a continent is evoked, it unites the identities of all those of African origin, no matter how temporally distant they might be from the moment of migration. The African imaginary is therefore quite complex and well developed, bringing together an extensive number of different voices and contributions to its ideation. The Asian imaginary, on the other hand, is not comparable. Shurik'N of the pioneering Marseillais rap group IAM is known for his love of Asia – in particular, Japan. Thus, his entire rap persona and the imagery surrounding it, that is manifested in visual and lyrical form in his music videos, speak to a construction of an Asian imaginary. There are a handful of such examples, but not more.

Moreover, where in this conception does the Middle East fall, or indeed, all the geographic spaces within which those who consider themselves or are considered to be Arabs are originally descended from? Geographically, the Arab identity straddles both Africa and Asia. In French rap and perhaps in France more generally, however, the Arab identity is once again defined on a macro level by its political realities. It is also distinct from other African and Asian imaginaries. In the case of Africa, there is a distinction of origin drawn between the Arab and the sub-Saharan collective identity. In the case of Asia, there are multiple fractures of identity that emerge with groups of countries bound together under distinct labels – the Middle East, Central Asia, South Asia, Southeast Asia, East Asia, etc. Yet the image of Asia in French rap is very much defined by, and associated with, the imaginary left in the wake of French colonialism. South Asians, for example, are nowhere to be seen in the narrative of French rap. To what extent those of Asian and African origins actually encounter each other outside of their musical imaginaries and in the real world is a question of space and reality. It is clear that Asians from the Middle East interact more often with those of African origin. Here, Islam also has a role to play in bringing about the coincidence of these differing groups through a shared commonality. There is a difference between what the rappers are saying/proposing and the national discourse, both of which promote (at differing moments) an image of tolerance and multiculturalism. In the case of rap, there is also another distinction to be made: most rappers in my selected archives elucidated experiences of marginalization based on a notion of difference from the norm (not always racial, but certainly always perceived), and thereby sought some kind of wider inclusivity, equality and greater tolerance. In short, the aspiration was for an openly embracing and multicultural France in reality and not just in rhetoric. However, some expressed it more particularly in relation to the groups which they, purposely or inadvertently, were representing – these could be ethnic, racial, linguistic, national (origin/descent) or any other – while others referred to an overall multicultural, multi-ethnic and multiracial image that included those who were not represented in any of those ways necessarily by the rapper himself (examples of the all-inclusive nature of the aspiration in rap quotes). In the latter case, those of (broader) Asian origin are included.

These are specific instances of reference to Asia in cultural rather than political terms. Although we might lament the absence of better development of an Asian imaginary with the same depth as the African imaginary, what is most significant about this lack is what it tells us about the nature of the encounters between the two imaginaries when they *do* coincide and interact. By and large, when African and Asian imaginaries meet, they do so because they must. Their shared challenge of existing in a society that does not (yet) consider them entirely its own has made them compatriots in quite a different way than they might have expected.

These nuances have made clear the most essential aspect of the encounter between African and Asian imaginaries in French rap: that when it comes to their political identities, there is a sense of unity and a common struggle to reprimand the society that posits itself as a universalist republic, but has, in the reality of their experiences, failed to realize these promises in practice. Though rappers of Asian origin are notably few in France in this time period, their communities are nevertheless spoken for. French rappers across time, space and artists have described a similar feeling of ostracism in a society that did not accept them as its own. This unintended concord is remarkable in a genre of music that does not require a governing idea or a manifesto as to its purpose. It resonates with eerie continuity not just in political thematic, but in identification of the problem (societal marginalization), the potential solution (appeal to the state) and the diction used to describe the social discontent. Dominant themes across time and artist include the contentious subjects of colonialism, immigration, discrimination, often in an associative form. This unexpected chorus, where a cacophony may have been more probable, gave French rap overall the true sense of a discourse, and made of rappers in France a set of representatives of an imagined community which was brought together by what they did not share and by what they were continually being denied – their rights and dues.

Thus, migrants in France are brought together not only by its geographic contours, but also by the physical spaces they share and, often, the social classes that these inadvertently define. Most of all, they share the periphery of societal existence. In other words, they are constantly ostracized by society for appearing to be 'incongruous' to what is practically accepted as the 'national norm' of the citizenry, even if this is nowhere clearly defined. France is the national space that provides the locus for these encounters between people of diverging and diverse origins. Although there is a fundamental aspiration to being French and integrating into the national space and imaginary, the reality of other identities brings complexity to this feeling of belonging that is echoed in the lyrics of rap songs in France. Rappers thus form a fascinating microcosm of at least one version of this ostracized 'other' in France, and their powerful and popular lyrical discourse provides a critical insight into the realities of those who wish to belong to the nation-state, but whom the nation-state does not consider its own (Ghose 2021). French rap's realism depicts a nation-state refusing to acknowledge the reality of its own portrait. Selective celebrations of multiculturalism, like the football World Cup, fuel the vision of a multicultural France, its people chorusing the slogan 'Black, Blanc, Beur' (Black, White, Arab) in unison. Yet the reality remains, as rapper Pit Baccardi puts it, *'Français quand on gagne, immigré quand on perd'* (French when we win, immigrants when we lose) – 'En Veux', 2007.

REFERENCES

Amiraux, V. and P. Simon (2006), 'There are no Minorities Here: Cultures of Scholarship and Public Debate on Immigrants and Integration in France', *International Journal of Comparative Sociology*, vol. 47, nos 3–4, pp. 191–215.

Austin, G. (2008), 'The "Reversal of Fortune" Thesis and the Compression of History: Perspectives from African and Comparative Economic History', *Journal of International Development*, vol. 20, no. 8, pp. 996–1027.

Bhambra, G.K. and J. Holmwood (2021), *Colonialism and Modern Social Theory*, Medford, MA: Polity Press.

Bleich, E. (2001), 'The French Model: Color-blind Integration', in J.D. Skrentny, ed., *Color Lines: Affirmative Action, Immigration, and Civil Rights Options for America*, Chicago: University of Chicago Press, pp. 270–96.

Comaroff, J. and J.L. Comaroff (2015), *Theory from the South: Or, How Euro-America is Evolving Toward Africa*, New York: Routledge.

Featherstone, M. (1990), 'Global Culture: An Introduction', *Theory, Culture & Society*, vol. 7, nos 2–3, pp. 1–14.

Frank, A.G. and B.K. Gills, eds (1996), *The World System: Five Hundred Years or Five Thousand?* London: Routledge.

Ghose, P. (2021), 'Rap Speaks, but Who Listens? The Musical "Other" in France', *History Workshop*, 4 January, available at https://www.historyworkshop.org.uk/music-sound/rap-speaks-but-who-listens/

Hammou, K. (2020), 'La Mémoire d'une Multitude: Techniques Musicales d'un Universalisme Minoritaire', Universalisme minoritaire, Working Paper.

Hargreaves, A.G. (2015), 'Empty Promises?: Public Policy against Racial and Ethnic Discrimination in France', *French Politics, Culture and Society*, vol. 33, no. 3, pp. 95–115.

INED (Institut National d'Études Démographiques) (2018), 'L'essentiel sur les Immigrés et les Étrangers'.

Niang, M-F. (2019), *Identités Françaises: Banlieues, Féminités et Universalisme*, Brill.

—— (2020), 'Des Particularités Françaises de la Négrophobie', in O. Slaouti and Olivier Le Cour Grandmaison, eds, *Racismes de France*, Paris: La Découverte, pp. 151–69.

Niang, M-F. and M. Soumahoro (2019), 'Du Besoin de Traduire et D'ancrer L'expérience Noire dans l'Hexagone', *Africultures*.

Seago, A. (2000), '"Where Hamburgers Sizzle on an Open Grill Night and Day"(?): Global Pop Music and Americanization in the Year 2000', *American Studies*, vol. 41, nos 2–3, pp. 119–36.

Silverman, M. (2002), *Deconstructing the Nation: Immigration, Racism and Citizenship in Modern France*, London: Routledge.

Slaouti, O. and Olivier Le Cour Grandmaison, eds (2020), *Racismes de France*, Paris: La Découverte.

7

The Drumming Tradition of South India

With Special Reference to Kerala's Percussion Art Forms

MANOJ KUROOR

The southern part of India has a rich tradition of percussion instruments as well as instrumental music. Among the percussion instruments, the mridangam, ganchira and ghatam share a common platform in the various states of south India, for they are popularly used as accompaniment in south Indian classical music, known as Karnatic music. Thavil is another instrument that accompanies the nagaswara, a wind instrument used in performances in south Indian states as a part of temple festivals and marriage ceremonies. South India also has a wonderful tradition of folk art forms, in many of which various types of percussion instruments are used.

Parai, an ancient drum which is depicted in *Tolkappiyam* and other Sangam works of ancient Tamil, had many forms – such as patalaparai, akuliparai, kiniparai, neytalparai, etc. – and they were practised by the Panar community in many art forms of that period. The instruments muzhavu and thannumai are two other major examples. We see the use of many different percussion instruments like maddalam, chenda, mizhavu, thappu, udukku, thudi, pampai and veeranam in different phases of south Indian history. Veeranam, a kind of war drum, is still present in the *veeranatya* of Andhra Pradesh. Another instrument, thaasa, which has a strong connection with northern India, is also used in the *veeranatya* dance form. Runja is a rare instrument of Telangana. It is interesting to see that the burraveena of Telangana, a stringed instrument by nature, is played like a percussion instrument for performances. By contrast, the idaykka of Kerala, which is basically a percussion instrument, can produce musical notes like a stringed instrument. Different types of parai are popular in the folk performances of Tamil Nadu and Karnataka. Chenda, the major percussion instrument present in many art forms of Kerala, gets prominence in *Yakshagana*, a dance-drama performed in Karnataka. Pampaimelam is a special form of percussion prevalent in Tamil Nadu as well as Kerala.

These are examples which depict the role and place of percussion instruments in the various performance traditions of south India. As far as percussion is concerned, Kerala boasts a number of orchestral forms and percussion occupies a more important position than vocal music in this southern Indian state. It must be noted that Kerala also has a vast oral tradition comprising a range of folk songs, such as *sopanasangeetham, kalamezhuthupattu, pulluvanpattu* and *mappilappattu*. But none of these musical forms have been attributed the status of classical art. However, this is not the case with percussive art forms in Kerala, which come in a wide variety of independent and stylized genres.

RHYTHMIC VARIETY OF *CHENDAMELAM*

*Chendamelam*s in different *tala*s (rhythms), such as *panchari, champata, champa, atantha, anchatantha* and *dhruvam*, are the major orchestral forms which are performed during temple festivals in Kerala. Chenda, the main instrument used in these *melam*s, is a cylindrical drum which has two sides. The batter head is known as *idanthala* and the resonant head is known as *valanthala*. Usually, percussionists play the chenda only on one side: either on the batter head or on the resonant head.

Four sounds can be produced from the batter head:

(1) The *di* sound is produced when the drum stick held in the right hand strikes the middle of the drumhead.

(2) The *na* sound is produced when the drum stick held in the right hand strikes the side of the drumhead.

(3) The *gi* sound is produced by beating the left hand in the middle of the drumhead.

(4) The *kam-kam* sound is produced by beating the left hand on the side of the drumhead.

A special way of drumming is *urulukai*, which means 'rolling hand'. While playing *urulukai*, the wrist of the right hand is moved inwards and outwards on the chenda. This method helps the drummer to play the chenda at any speed.

Chendamelam is a collective performance by more than a hundred artists using various musical instruments, but the chenda is the most prominent. *Valanthala* chenda, kurunkuzhal, kombu and ilathalam are the other instruments played in a *chendamelam*. *Valanthala*, the resonant head of the chenda, is used to count the rhythm beats and keep the tempo. Kurunkuzhal and kombu, traditional wind instruments, are exploited to add charm to the percussive patterns. There is a definite proportion in which all these instruments are used in every *melam*: chenda, kurunkuzhal and kombu are used in equal number; the number of ilathalam should be double the number of chenda; and the number of *valanthala* should be three times the number of chenda.

Though the musical ensemble is the same, the rhythms and succession of tempos are different for every *melam*. *Pancharimelam*, with five tempos, is the most popular among these orchestral forms. *Panchari tala* is the basic rhythm performed by progressively accelerating from the first tempo of 96 *matras* (beats) to the fifth tempo of 6 *matras*. The second, third and fourth tempos consist of 48, 24 and 12 *matras*, respectively. Each tempo is divided into three phases, known as the *nerkol* phase, *thakkitta* phase and *kuzhamarinja* phase. The rhythm pattern of *pancharimelam* is given below. Letters like *thi* and *dhim* represent various sounds produced on the *valanthala*; 'x' indicates the silent interval between sounds.

(1) First tempo: 96 beats
thi x *thi* x *thi* x *thi* x *thi* x *thi* x *thi* x x x
thi x *thi* x *thi* x x x *thi* x *thi* x *thi* x x x
thi x *thi* x *thi* x x x *thi* x *thi* x *thi* x x x
thi x *thi* x *thi* x *thi* x *dhim* x *dhim* x *dhim* x x x
thi x *thi* x *thi* x *thi* x *thi* x *thi* x *thi* x x x
thi x *thi* x *thi* x *thi* x *thi* x *thi* x *thi* x x x
thi x *thi* x *thi* x *thi* x *thi* x *thi* x *thi* x x x
thi x *thi* x *thi* x *thi* x *dhim* x *dhim* x *dhim* x x x
thi x *thi* x *thi* x *thi* x *thi* x *thi* x *thi* x x x
thi x *thi* x *thi* x *thi* x *dhim* x *dhim* x *dhim* x x x
dhim x x x *dhim* x x x *dhim* x x x *dhim* x x *dhim*
x x *dhim* x *dhim* x *dhim* x *dhim* x *dhim* x *dhim* x x x

(2) Second tempo: 48 beats
thi x *thi* x *thi* x x x *thi* x x x *thi* x x x
thi x x x *thi* x *thi* x *dhim* x *dhim* x *dhim* x x x
thi x *thi* x *thi* x *thi* x *dhim* x *dhim* x *dhim* x x x
thi x *thi* x *thi* x *thi* x *dhim* x *dhim* x *dhim* x x x
thi x *thi* x *thi* x *thi* x *dhim* x *dhim* x *dhim* x x *dhim*
x x *dhim* x *dhim* x *dhim* x *dhim* x *dhim* x *dhim* x x x

(3) Third tempo: 24 beats
thi x *thi* x *thi* x *thi* x *dhim* x *dhim* x *dhim* x x x
dhim x *dhim* x *dhim* x x x *dhim* x *dhim* x *dhim* x x *dhim*
x x *dhim* x *dhim* x *dhim* x *dhim* x *dhim* x *dhim* x x x

(4) Fourth tempo: 12 beats
thi x *thi* x *dhim* x x x *dhim* x x x
dhim x x x *dhim* x *dhim* x *dhim* x x x

(5) Fifth tempo: 6 beats
dhim x *dhim* x *dhim* x *dhim* x *dhim* x x x

Pancharimelam represents the stylization that could apply to a simple rhythm which is in the form of five beats followed by one interval. The first tempo of this *melam* is divided into twelve parts and each part contains eight beats. Then the total number of beats is 96. The second tempo is divided into six parts, the third tempo into three parts, the fourth tempo into twelve beats, and the final tempo manifests the basic form of the *panchari tala*. Other *melams* like *champata, champa, atantha* and *anchatantha* are performed in four tempos, but the rare *melamdhruvam* has three tempos only. All these *melams* are known by the name of the specific rhythm used in them. The basic form of each rhythm is given below.

(1) *champata: thi thi thi thi dhim* x *dhim* x (eight beats)

(2) *champa: thi thi thi dhim* x *dhim dhim* x *dhim* x (ten beats)

(3) *atantha: thi thi thi dhim* x *thi thi thi dhim* x *dhim* x *dhim* x (fourteen beats)

(4) *anchatantha: thi thi thi thi dhim* x *thi thi thi thi dhim* x *dhim* x *dhim* x (sixteen beats)

(5) *dhruvam: thi* x *thi* x *thi* x *thi* x *dhim* x x *dhim* x x *dhim* x *dhim* x *dhim* x *dhim* x *dhim* x *dhim* x x x (fourteen beats)

There is a popular *melam* known as *pandimelam* which is very different from the other *melams* in its rhythm pattern and succession of tempos. The rhythm of this *melam* is calculated as multiples of seven beats. Even though the basic form of the rhythm is the same, there are slight variations in the sound patterns of each tempo. The rhythmic patterns of some different tempos of *pandimelam* are given below:

(1) *dhim* x x x *thi* x *thi* x *thi* x *thi* x *dhim* x x *dhim* x x *dhim* x *dhim* x *dhim* x *dhim* x *dhim* x

(2) *dhim* x x x *dhim* x x x *dhim* x x x *dhim* x x *dhim* x x *dhim* x *dhim* x *dhim* x *dhim* x *dhim* x

(3) *dhim* x x *dhim* x x *dhim* x x *dhim* x x *dhim* x x *dhim* x x *dhim* x *dhim* x x x *dhim* x *dhim* x

(4) *dhim* x x x *dhi* x *dhim* x x x *dhi* x *dhi* x

(5) *dhim* x *dhim* *dhim* *dhim* *dhim* *dhim*

In all of these percussive art forms, rhythm plays a significant role by changing its form in each tempo, and this complex structure of rhythmic succession makes the whole performance memorable and splendid. *Champata*, a simple rhythm consisting of eight *matras*, which is similar to *aadi tala* of Karnatic music, takes the form of 64 beats in the first tempo of *champatamelam*. The second tempo is in thirty-two *matras* and the third tempo performs in sixteen *matras*. The original form of the rhythm appears only in the last tempo. That means, the way of counting beats in each tempo is different, because of the dependence on percussion instruments and cymbals for this purpose instead of hand actions (*hastakriyas*), as is popular in classical vocal music. Similarly, *champa tala* of ten *matras* not only varies in the *matras* of every tempo, but keeps a difference in rhythm structure also. Though *atantha tala* and *dhruva tala* share the same number of fourteen *matras*, the structures of these *melams* are different. *Anchatantha tala* of sixteen *matras* resembles *champata tala* in the number of *matras*, but each of these *melams* retains its own identity in the method of percussion. Though the percussion instruments and method of percussion are different in *panchavadyam* and *pandimelam*, both these orchestral forms have a similarity in the number of *matras* in the parallel phases of rhythm succession, so to speak, and these phases are set in the *matras* containing multiples of seven. *Panchavadyam* allows space for individual improvisation also.

THAYAMPAKA: THE ART OF PERSONAL IMPROVISATION

Thayampaka, another percussion art form which presents chenda as its main instrument, contrasts with the *melam* tradition by keeping its unique form as an independent improvisation. The starting rhythm of *thayampaka* is *champata* and the first part of the performance is known as *champatavattom*. It starts in a slow tempo and steadily progresses through different phases like *kooru*, *idanila* and *irikida*. There are three types of *kooru*: *pancharikooru*, *champakooru* and *atanthakooru*. All these *koorus* are not presented in a single performance. Usually, the main drummer presents either *pancharikooru* followed by *champakooru*, or *adanthakooru* alone. After presenting the *kooru*, *thayampaka* performance enters into the next phase, named *idanila*. Finally set afoot in a full-tilt tempo of *irikida* phase, it excites the mass audience of a temple festival. *Keli* and *maddalappattu*, the other two art forms, are similar to *thayampaka* in some phases of the performance. The rhythm patterns in the different phases of *thayampaka* are given below.

(1) *champata* in slow tempo: *dhim* x x x x x x x *dhim* x x x *dhim* x *dhim dhim*

(2) *champata* in fast tempo: *dhim* x x x *dhim* x *dhim dhim*

(3) *pancharikooru*: *dhim* x x *tha* x x *tha* x x *tha* x x *dhim* x x *tha* x x *dhim* x x *dhim* x x

(4) *champakooru*: *dhim* x *tha tha* x / *tha* x *tha tha* x / *tha* x *tha tha* x / *tha* x *tha tha* x / *dhim* x *tha tha* x / *tha* x *tha tha* x / *dhim* x *tha tha* x / *dhim* x *tha tha* x / *dhim* x *dhi dhim* x

(5) *atanthakooru*: *dhim* x x *tha* x *tha* x/ *dhim* x x *tha* x *tha* x/ *dhim* x x *tha* x *tha* x/ *dhim* x x *tha* x *tha* x

(6) *itanila* and *irikida*: *dhim* x

PANCHAVADYAM: A UNIQUE RHYTHMIC STRUCTURE

Panchavadyam is another kind of musical orchestra performed in Kerala. The main instrument played in *panchavadyam* is *thimila*. *Maddalam, idaykka, kombu, ilathalam* and *sankhu* are the other instruments involved in this art form. The rhythm succession of *panchavadyam* is different from that of *chendamelam*. It starts with a very slow tempo that consists of 896 *matras*, progressively changes to different phases and ends in a rapid tempo of three-and-a-half *matras*. A popular legend about the origin of *panchavadyam* says that the rhythm of this art form is in the pattern of a hymn: *mrityunjaya/harahara/sambho* (*dhimdhimthaka/thakathaka/dhimdhim*). This metrical form contains fourteen *matras*. Even though there are some slight differences in the contemporary practice of *panchavadyam*, this metrical pattern suggests that each rhythm cycle can be divided into three prominent parts. The first part contains six *matras*, and the second and third parts have four *matras* each (6 + 4 + 4). The fifth tempo of *panchavadyam* represents the basic structure of this art form and the rhythm cycle of that stage contains 56 *matras*, which can be divided into three parts as 24 + 16 + 16. The total number of 56 *matras* can be subdivided once again into twelve parts. The rhythm pattern of this phase is given below.

(1) *dhi* x *tha ka* / *tha ka tha ka* / *tha ka tha ka* / *tha ka tha ka* / *tha ka tha ka* / *tha ka tha ka* / *tha ka tha ka* / *tha ka dhim* x / (8 *matras*)

(2) x x *tha ka* / *tha ka tha ka* / *tha ka tha ka* / *tha ka dhim* x / (4 *matras*)

(3) x x *tha ka* / *tha ka tha ka* / *tha ka tha ka* / *tha ka dhim* x / (4 *matras*)

(4) x x *tha ka* / *tha ka tha ka* / *tha ka tha ka* / *tha ka tha ka* / *tha ka tha ka* / *tha ka tha ka* / *tha ka tha ka* / *tha ka dhim* x / (8 *matras*)

Here ends the first part of twenty-four *matras*. The fourth part is known as *koottipperukkam*.

(5) x x *tha ka* / *tha ka dhim* x / (2 *matras*)

(6) x x *tha ka* / *tha ka dhim* x / (2 *matras*)

(7) x x *tha ka* / *tha ka dhim* x / (2 *matras*)

(8) x x *tha ka* / *tha ka dhim* x / (2 *matras*)

(9) *tha ka tha ka* / *tha ka tha ka* / *tha ka tha ka* / *tha ka tha ka* / *dhim* x *tha ka* / *tha* x *dhim* x / x x *tha ka* / *tha ka tha* x / (8 *matras*)

Here is the end of the second part of 16 *matras*. This phase is known as *vakram*.

(10) x x *thaka* / *tha ka tha ka* / *thakathaka* / *thakathaka* / *dhim*x *tha ka* /*tha* x *dhim* x /x x *thaka* /*tha ka tha* x / (8 *matras*)

(11) *dhim*xx x / x x *thaka* / *tha ka tha ka* / (3 *matras*)

(12) *dhim*xx x / x x *thaka* / *tha ka tha* x / *tha ka tha ka* / *dhim* x *tha* x / (5 *matras*)

The rhythm cycle ends here. This final part is known as *kalaasam*. In this way, the first five tempos can be divided into three parts. The division of *matras* in each tempo is given below.

First tempo:	384	+ 256	+ 256	= 896
Second tempo:	192	+ 128	+ 128	= 448
Third tempo:	96	+ 64	+ 64	= 224
Fourth tempo:	48	+ 32	+ 32	= 112
Fifth tempo:	24	+ 16	+ 16	= 56

The sixth tempo is a phase of transformation to the next stages. It contains twenty-eight *matras*. The rhythm pattern of this phase, which can be considered as the next tempo, is depicted on *ilathalam* as follows:

Sixth tempo: *thi thi thi thi thei* x / *thi thi thi thi thei* x / *thi thi thi thi thi thei* x / *thi thi thi thi thi thei* x /; division of *matras*: 6 + 6 + 8 + 8 = 28.

This pattern repeats three times with varying speed each time. This phase is exclusive in this manner. The next two tempos are known as *thriputa*.

Seventh tempo (first *thriputa*): *thi thi thi thi thei* x / *thi thi thei* x / *thi thi thei* x /; division of *matras*: 6 + 4 + 4 = 14.

Eighth tempo (second *thriputa*): *thi thei* x / *thi thi thei* x /; division of *matras*: 3 + 4 = 7.

When *panchavadyam* enters into the final phase, the tempo accelerates again from seven *matras* to three-and-a-half *matras* and transforms to another rhythm, *eka tala*. The performance culminates with some improvisations done by the group of *thimila* artists.

There are some other percussion art forms that are performed as a part of temple rituals. *Panikottu* is an example. *Kombupattu*, a performance on the *kombu*, a wind instrument, gives more attention to *tala* than tonal improvisation. *Dufmuttu* and *arabanamuttu* are performed by the Muslim community in the Malabar region of Kerala. *Thappumelam*, a percussive art performed on an instrument called *thappu*, associated with a ritual art form *padayani*, has a special mode of performance. This is popular in southern Kerala.

The art forms of Kerala have given more attention to percussion than to tonal music in general. This propensity is reflected in the stylization of percussive art forms. Four- to five-hour-long percussive performances are very common in the temple festivals of Kerala. Whether it is *chendamelam* or *panchavadyam*, the performance starts at a very slow first tempo and ends in rapid tempo. The specific way of presentation, which combines indigenous rhythmic patterns, appeals to the audience irrespective of class divisions. The *pièce de résistance* of this culture demands more attention from music lovers all over the world.

Contributors

Mark Aranha is a musician and musicologist from New Delhi. His research around the music and history of Jews and Mappilas of Kerala formed the basis of his Master's degree at the University of Cape Town. He has worked as a performer and composer across India and South Africa in a variety of genres from jazz and pop to traditional Indian and Xhosa music.

Sumangala Damodaran is an economist, musician and composer with over three decades of teaching experience at Dr. B.R. Ambedkar University Delhi and Delhi University. As a labour economist, her work covers the informal economy, migration, gender and global value chains. She has also done extensive research and document-ation in music, with notable publications such as *The Radical Impulse: Music and Politics in the IPTA Tradition* and the album *Songs of Protest*. She is a co-founder of the award-winning transcontinental Indian–South African collaboration, Insurrections Ensemble, and a large multi-institutional project on music and migration which has resulted in a book, *Maps of Sorrow*, co-authored with Ari Sitas.

Kathyayini Dash is an art practitioner and academic scholar. She teaches at Ahmedabad University in the Performing and Visual Arts

Division, School of Arts and Sciences. She is interested in multi-disciplinary approaches to research and art-making practices. Her work has centred around studying affect, embodied knowledges and histories that emerge out of artistic research methodologies. She has written, presented and performed her work across a range of multi-disciplinary platforms, her most recent contributions being to the Re-centring AfroAsia project: Musical and Human Migrations in the Pre-Colonial Period (700 to 1500 AD). Other recent works have been shown at the Mardin Biennial V Turkey, and at the Center for Theatre Dance and Performance Studies, University of Cape Town.

Sazi Dlamini is an ethnomusicologist and a senior research associate of the Re-centring AfroAsia project. In 1991, he founded SKOKIANA – an ensemble of jazz-influenced South African black township music; he is a member of the transcontinental 'Insurrections Ensemble'. He has interest in musical bows of eastern South Africa and is editor of *Musical Bows of Southern Africa* (2020). He holds a PhD degree from the University of KwaZulu-Natal for his thesis titled 'South African Blue Notes: Bebop, Mbaqanga, Apartheid and the Exiling of a Musical Imagination'.

Paroma Ghose holds a PhD degree from the Department of International History, Graduate Institute of International and Development Studies (IHEID), Geneva. Her doctoral research looked at the experience of the 'outsider' and the notion of belonging in France (1981–2012) through the lyrics of French rap songs. She was awarded the Pierre du Bois Prize for the best doctoral thesis in international history at IHEID in 2020. She is currently an affiliated researcher at the Graduate Institute and a fellow of the Pierre du Bois Foundation for current history. She is the author of 'Le Point d'Interrogation', a bilingual blog, with the Swiss newspaper *Le Temps*.

Luis Gimenez Amoros is a research fellow at the Global South Studies Center, University of Cologne. Previously, he has served as a music and cultural anthropology lecturer in South Africa, Malaysia and Brazil. His academic research focuses on music and refugees in the Sahara Desert (for his doctoral dissertation), sound repatriation and revitalization of historical recordings from African sound archives, and the historical circulation of Iberian music within an AfroAsian context and in Latin America. His publications include the monograph *Tracing the Mbira Sound Archive in Zimbabwe* (2018) and the award-winning album series, 'The Unknown Spanish Levant', recorded in Germany, Egypt, Brazil, Mexico, Malaysia, South Africa, Turkey and Spain.

Nkosenathi Ernie Koela is an initiated healer and PhD candidate specializing in indigenous music therapies at the University of Cape Town. Koela's transdisciplinary practice encompasses being an Afrikan indigenous sound medium, artist, specialist and teacher. As an instrument maker and multi-instrumentalist, Koela explores how healing practices through sound create space that manifests spiritually and materially.

Manoj Kuroor teaches Malayalam in NSS College, Pandalam, Kerala. He is a well-known poet, composer and fiction writer in Malayalam, and has won several awards and recognition for his writing. Apart from his creative writing, he is an excellent percussionist of chenda and plays the instrument for Kathakali performances. He has written more than fifty articles on topics such as western classical music, classical art forms, popular music, folklore art forms, cinema, literature and cyber culture.